Vagabondage

A Timeless Reaction to the Malignancy of Western Civilization

Ian Cutler

Series in Philosophy

Copyright © 2025 Vernon Press, an imprint of Vernon Art and Science Inc, on behalf of the author.

All rights reserved. No part of this publication may be reproduced, stored in a retrieval system, or transmitted in any form or by any means, electronic, mechanical, photocopying, recording, or otherwise, without the prior permission of Vernon Art and Science Inc.

www.vernonpress.com

In the Americas:
Vernon Press
1000 N West Street, Suite 1200
Wilmington, Delaware, 19801
United States

In the rest of the world:
Vernon Press
C/Sancti Espiritu 17,
Malaga, 29006
Spain

Series in Philosophy

Library of Congress Control Number: 2025932505

ISBN: 979-8-8819-0279-7

Also available: 979-8-8819-0239-1 [Hardback]; 979-8-8819-0278-0 [PDF, E-Book]

Product and company names mentioned in this work are the trademarks of their respective owners. While every care has been taken in preparing this work, neither the authors nor Vernon Art and Science Inc. may be held responsible for any loss or damage caused or alleged to be caused directly or indirectly by the information contained in it.

Cover design by Vernon Press.

Every effort has been made to trace all copyright holders, but if any have been inadvertently overlooked the publisher will be pleased to include any necessary credits in any subsequent reprint or edition.

Freedom is a consequence of relinquishing the material world.

Olivia Laing

For my wife Angela, who helped me become a writer, and my sons Seth and Max (and Angela too), who help me become a better human being

Ian Cutler's latest book, *Vagabondage: A Timeless Reaction to the Malignancy of Western Civilization,* follows earlier chroniclers of vagabondage (from Arthur Rickett to Stephen Graham) in offering a broad conception of the term as a philosophical outlook and way of life. Taking us on a whistle—stop tour, from Diogenes to Nietszche, Cutler itemises the defining attributes of this broad system of belief: from an inclination to wander to a tendency towards introspection; from an implicit childishness to a love of nature—with a central connecting disregard for the Platonic attributes of mainstream Western civilisation uniting the many authors subject to scrutiny. Cutler's book is an impassioned and idiosyncratic 'diatribe' (in true Cynic fashion) against the process of civilisation, offering insights into an eclectic array of dissenters, many of whom ... (in particular, the homeless writers that formed the subject of Cutler's *The Lives And Extraordinary Adventures Of Fifteen Tramp Writers From The Golden Age Of Vagabondage*) have been unfairly neglected. A valuable insight for those interested in vagabondage in its many cultural forms.

Dr Luke Davies,
Lecturer in Film Studies Keele University

Ian Cutler is the laureate of itinerants and loiterers. In his latest contribution to the literature on vagabonds, he offers not only an erudite compendium of tramping since ancient times but a characteristically thought-provoking, even moving meditation on what it means to feel, in one's legs and one's soul, that restless longing to be on the road. I learned a great deal from it and will return to it again and again.

Professor Matthew Beaumont,
Department of English Literature
University College London Gower Street

Anyone who wants to understand the vagabond as a core archetype of humanity can hardly do better than become a fellow traveller on Ian Cutler's magnificent journey across several millennia of tramping. This book will change your idea of what civilization and especially Western civilization means; it may also change your idea of what it means to be human.

Emeritus Professor Yiannis Gabriel,
Bath University, UK

Ian Cutler expertly and impressively covers a staggering amount of literary and philosophical territory in "Vagabondage: A Timeless Reaction to the Malignancy of Western Civilization." He [Cutler] deftly explores a wide range of aspects to this challenging and complex subject, insightfully probing the mighty depths beneath this fascinating territory. Along the way, he puts you in such celebrated company as Robert Louis Stevenson, Jack London, Virginia Woolf, Charles Dickens and Jack Kerouac, as well as some rovers and writers whose words are lesser known but no less valuable. Throughout this odyssey, Cutler remains our able guide, pointing out the common themes that have shaped and defined vagabond literature.

Mark Dawidziak

Ian Cutler is the greatest living authority on the now almost extinct tramp writer. In this beautifully written and scholarly analysis of the philosophy of male and female literary vagabondage he traces the genre's roots back to the Cynics.

Reading it made me want to pack my rucksack and escape from the noisy buzzing of the human zoo and tramp the rolling road leaving my cares and obligations behind me.

Professor Andrew Lees,
University College London

TABLE OF CONTENTS

	PREFACE	xi
	INTRODUCTION: THE BEGINNINGS OF VAGABONDAGE AS A PHILOSOPHY	xvii
Chapter 1	WANDERLUST	1
Chapter 2	AFFINITY WITH NATURE	15
Chapter 3	THE URBAN VAGABOND	27
Chapter 4	THE LONE AND LOFTY PERCH OF WORLD-HATING INTROSPECTION	43
Chapter 5	PETER PAN SYNDROME	53
Chapter 6	FACT or FICTION?	65
Chapter 7	THE VAGABOND TEMPERAMENT	77
	REFERENCES	83

PREFACE

In this volume, I have departed from my usual biographical mode of writing to pen what could be described as an anthological essay on vagabondage: anthological in as much as in many instances, around half of the words printed come directly from the original authors, over 50 of whom are now fortunately out of copyright.

As often happens after publishing a monograph, you discover another that you wish you'd come across while still writing the first. Following the publication of my biography of fifteen tramp writers in 2020, I came across four other texts on the subject of Vagabond Literature (and, of course, many other primary texts by vagabond writers). The first two, Kerri Andrews, *Wanderers: A History of Women Walking* (2020) and Luke Lewin Davies' *The Tramp in British Literature, 1850–1950* (2022), were not available to me at the time of writing this book. But there was no excuse for not locating the other two, published over 100 years ago: Arthur Rickett's *The Vagabond in Literature* (1906) and Hilaire Belloc's *The Footpath Way* (1911). Both these latter texts introduce the writing and philosophy of well-known writers with the vagabond instinct including, among others, William Hazlitt, H. D. Thoreau, George Borrow, Thomas de Quincy, Walt Whitman and R. L. Stevenson. Andrews' book is particularly important as these earlier texts neglected important women writers on the subject. Be that as it may, on reading both Rickett and Andrew's books, I was delighted to discover that their focus was, as with my own work, on the vagabond writer, not the vagabond as a fictional character. It was partly these texts that prompted me to write this current volume for reasons I will explain.

The main distinction between my work and Rickett's, was less the separation of 119 years in which they were published—although that provided its own fascination—so much as that the vagabond writers who were the subject of his book (and, for that matter Belloc and Andrew's also) were, and for the most part still are today, household names in the world of literature. This is an important if not slightly artificial distinction, best described by the writer Emily Burbank (1908, p. 346) when she commented on Josiah Flynt, one of the writers in my 2020 text, "it must be remembered that Flynt was the tramp writing, not the literary man tramping" I used this definition in selecting the fifteen chapters of my previous book because, with the possible exception of Jack London, I was interested in rescuing what I regarded as forgotten writers from obscurity and, as with Burbank's definition, wanted to consider tramps who were drawn to writing (even if some of them undoubtedly sought literary success) rather than celebrated writers who tramped to inspire their writing. For the purpose of this current text, I will refer to the former as 'tramp writers' to distinguish them from 'literary vagabonds,' the other species of vagabond philosophers cited in this book. When discussing both groups as one, I will use the term 'vagabond writer.' In his book, *Paris Vagabond* (discussed in Chapter 3), Jean-Paul Clébert (2016, p. 50) makes a similar distinction between those two groups when he refers to the 'vagabond poet' and the 'poet vagabond.' But, as I've already acknowledged, in reality, there is very little real distinction because both categories of vagabonds were driven by the same urges and shared the same philosophy of living in both the 'human' world and the 'natural' world—the former being frequently described as 'unnatural' by ancient and modern vagabond writers throughout this text. It should also be noted that most of the texts that appear in this book, from all of the writers referred to above, were written approximately between 1850 and 1950.

The other reason for writing this book was that I had been contacted by someone who had read my two biographies on tramp writers and suggested that I should write another, less biographical work; one which examined the phenomenon of vagabond literature along the common philosophical themes (wanderlust, affinity with nature, the abject, cosmopolitanism, etcetera) that were clearly emerging from the writing. I touched on these in the final chapter of an earlier book, *Jim Christy: A Vagabond Life* (2019), but never fully developed them. On discovering that the writers featured by Rickett, Belloc and Andrews had all written with passion on these same topics, I needed no further persuasion to start writing this present volume, here sparked by the following challenge laid down by Rickett (1906, p. 84):

> It is idle to seek for the literary parentage of this Vagabond. Better far to accept him as he is, a wanderer, a rover, a curious taster of life, at once a mystic and a realist. He may have qualities that repel; but so full is he of contradictions that no sooner has the frown settled on the brow than it gives place to a smile. We may not always like him; never can we ignore him.

Earlier in his book, Rickett raised another question concerning the progenitor of the vagabond, one not unrelated to their "literary parentage": is the vagabond born or made a vagabond? I have attempted to answer this latter question at the end of Chapter 1, but as for the vagabond writers' literary parentage, an attempt to identify this is covered by the Introduction that follows. As for the remaining chapters in this book, each addresses a principle theme of vagabondage, presented for the most part by the words of vagabond writers themselves. This will include the thoughts and ideas of the ancient Greek Cynics and the vagabond culture of the early Jesus movement (as distinct from its corruption as Christianity), as these probably represent the first organized doctrines identifying what could be described as a philosophy of vagabondage in response to the suffocating glue of morality that has dominated Western Civilization since its early beginnings—and of which Christianity (along with science, the judiciary, etcetera) would become one of the principal contributors and guardians of its 'truths.'

Before getting into the central arguments of this book, it is worth making clear some of the subjects that this book does *not* cover, even if such material would provide excellent subjects for other books, and, indeed, is referred to in many of the books cited. This book is restricted to a discussion of vagabondage as discussed by those who left—mainly prose—accounts of their adventures, lifestyle and philosophy. It is not a book about homelessness, migrant workers, or the general lifestyle of the hobo.

Of course, there were occasions when most of the 'tramp writers' cited in this text *did* engage with conventional society, and worked—or starved. In my biography of fifteen tramp writers, there are many detailed accounts of the varied work that they engage with, and, in many cases, excelled. As the modern-day vagabond writer, Jim Christy, says in his forthcoming book *Keep on Working* (2025): "It should be emphasized that tramps were not bums. They walked and would work if it was necessary, whereas hoboes rode freights and actively sought work". For anyone interested in the working life of tramps (and also of circus and carnival performers) and of Christy's own fascinating and entertaining list of jobs in particular, I recommend a reading of *Keep on Working*.

In contrast to the tramp writer, the 'literary vagabonds' cited in this text were, of course, professional writers by trade. Even some of the aforementioned tramp writers went on to publish successfully after, or during, a life on the road; many also engaged in paid journalistic activities. Some vagabond writers came from wealthy families or families who were deeply involved in the very society that the vagabond writer rejected. I emphasise again, this is not a book about economic migrants who led a vagabond lifestyle out of necessity. It is about those who engaged in vagabondage as a personal philosophy and a deliberate lifestyle choice.

Most of the vagabond writers discussed in this text describe their lifestyle in terms of this strategic way of thinking and of being in the world. Cutting themselves off from mainstream society, both physically and emotionally. This in no way prevented them from engaging in conventional ways with the rest of society when the occasion demanded, including, as already mentioned, working. But this book will focus on the vagabond features of its subjects, not conventional aspects of life they may have engaged in.

When I refer later to the view that the vagabond did not try to persuade others to their point of view, or generally identify with others as a tribe, this is a characteristic that, in most cases, is easy to support. It is true that there were organizations associated with hoboism, such as the Industrial Workers of the World (IWW or Wobblies), however, although embracing members with no regular workplace, this was primarily a politically motivated group concerned with labor activism. It sought to recruit economic migrants, rather than vagabonds of choice, to their cause. As Todd DePastino identifies in his book *Citizen Hobo* (2003, p. 111), the IWW's "primary task was to spread revolutionary propaganda". In his book *The Tramp in America*, Tim Cresswell (2001, p. 196) identifies that those hobos primarily recruited by the IWW ("semi-successfully," he adds) were migrant workers, "bindle stiffs" or "fruit tramps."

Therefore, the IWW cannot represent a collective identity for the literary vagabonds who are the subject of this book. As Douglas Harper noted in *Good Company: A Tramp Life* (1982, p. 153): "The tramp remains free of and unrepentant to a society which he perceives as a set of pressure to conform, to take orders, and to be unadventuresome." These rules and conformities applied as much to the IWW and similar political organizations (even if they may have been associated with hobos) as they did to the rest of mainstream society. This includes the anarchist movement, which, although they may share similar attitudes to government and their institutions, have an organized political agenda which most vagabonds do not.

At the end of Chapter 4, 'The Lone and Lofty Perch of World-Hating Introspection,' I discuss in more detail the vagabond's relationship to society at large and why I claim that vagabondage was not associated with any organized movement but was rather a loosely shifting social web of individuals who, while they may sometimes share spaces and agendas, stood very much outside of conventional society, its rules and its prohibitions.

I have also acknowledged the scarcity of tramp literature by women and, in spite of much research, was only able to find and include the work of one in my biography of fifteen such writers—that is, 'tramp writers', as opposed to the women 'literary vagabonds' who feature in Andrews' book and are discussed further below. But why do no non-white vagabond writers appear in this text, in particular African-Americans, who accounted for around 10% of American hobos, according to Iain McIntyre, in his book *On the Fly* (2018). It is a question I get asked, and so I will deal with it here, but if any of my readers are aware of vagabond literature by writers of non-European heritage, I would very much appreciate hearing from them.

I acquired McIntyre's book, and other texts, in the hope of discovering some writing by African-American vagabonds. *On the Fly* is an anthology of stories, songs and poetry from 85 hobo writers, yet only two of these are identified as African-Americans by name (there are several blues songs of anonymous origin). These were Henry Thomas and Bumble Bee Slim, and in both cases, the songs were simply accounts of riding freight trains with nothing to describe the lifestyle of their writers or others they encountered (McIntyre, 2018, pp. 377 and 461).

McIntyre claims that although millions of African Americans migrated North following the Civil War, they mostly traveled on passenger trains because of the combination of racism and the harsh vagrancy laws used in the South to jail ex-slaves as a means to allow private industry to exploit their labor via "convict lease" schemes. The few who did beat freight trains, McIntyre adds, often "included blues musicians who hopped boxcars to perform in juke joints and clubs, as well as on street corners" (2018, p. 3). DePastino also noted the limitations to tramping by African Americans, reinforced after the Civil War by Southern power brokers seeking to maintain their cheap labor supply through debt peonage and draconian vagrancy laws. DePastino adds that: "Without the right to move on their own terms, African Americans were effectively barred from the privileges of tramping" (2003, p. 14). DePastino (2003, p. 14) further noted that, "few poor African Americans dared to step foot on the road. The black aversion to tramping is attributable not only to outright racial discrimination in public assistance, but also to the hostility and violence that blacks could expect to encounter on the road itself".

Acknowledging that racism was openly practiced in all aspects of American life during the late nineteenth and early twentieth centuries, including the hobo community itself; with the exception of Dolly Kennedy Yancy, discussed in Chapter 1, there is no evidence that any of the vagabond writers featured in this text displayed any racist views or opinions. Indeed, in stark contrast to the prevailing attitudes of the time, there were many accounts of close friendships between white and non-white vagabonds. This is further reinforced by the vagabond writers' cosmopolitan lifestyle and philosophy—discussed in detail in Chapter 4—which contrasted deeply with the prevailing prejudices of mainstream society of the time.

And what of Native Americans? Like Australian Aboriginals and other nomadic peoples across the globe, they were victims of the most dramatic effects of the malignancy of the West's 'civilizing' and Christianizing processes? The lifestyle and traditions of Native Americans often provided inspiration for the vagabond—as will be discussed later. Native Americans had lived in harmony with the natural world for countless millennia, not 'owning' the land they inhabited (in the way the European immigrants developed and held 'property rights'), not building permanent dwelling places, and not encumbering themselves with more possessions than was absolutely necessary to meet their day to day needs, they simply lived on what the earth provided. This included herds of buffalo, often up to 100,000 strong (Hickman, 2022, p. 319), that also freely roamed the plains and provided Native Americans with meat for food and hide for their footwear, clothing and tipis. Yet in only three decades during the mid-1800s, the westward expansion of white (and black) immigrants, fuelled by the discovery of gold, by the expansion of the railways, and by financial crashes in the East that encouraged pioneers to seek new land in which to settle, the Native American's traditional way of life was finally ended. Exposed to a series of broken treaties and genocidal acts, supported and sometimes promoted by successive United States administrations, those who were not killed (or starved as the buffalo population they depended on was also nearing extinction) were forced onto reservations where their former nomadic lifestyle was finally ended (Hickman, 2022, p. 341).

INTRODUCTION:
THE BEGINNINGS OF VAGABONDAGE AS A PHILOSOPHY

The fact is, all man's ingenuity and advances in technology were, at best, mixed blessings in the lives of later generations. ... And in this single-minded pursuit, their lives actually became less pleasant and more oppressive; their devotion to self-interest brought them to dreadful ends.

Dio Chrysostom (c. 40 – c. 115 AD), *6th Oration* (cited in Dobbin, 2012, p. 97)

Man is more of a man in the social state that is called savage and uncivilised. Civilisation is but a vast, theatric, backward step in the social life of humanity.

Bart Kennedy, *A Tramp's Philosophy* (1908, p. 249)

There can be no mistake. Civilisation has increased man's producing power a hundred-fold, and through mismanagement the men of Civilisation live worse than the beasts [...] If Civilisation has increased the producing power of the average man, why has it not bettered the lot of the average man?

Jack London, *People of the Abyss* (1903)

There are thousands of vagabonds on the earth, but, as noted above, for the purposes of this little book, I want to refer to those who were or are vagabonds by choice rather than vagabonds of circumstance. I will further limit my informants to those vagabonds who have left some commentary on their relationship with mainstream Western society, in particular, those whose vagabond lifestyle was defined by the strategies they employed to live a life free from the tyranny and constraints they felt from society's laws and conventions.

To further contextualize the book's title, I date the birth of 'Western Civilization' to the battle for Socrates' inheritance from around 450 BCE onwards. Having said which, the term has become somewhat meaningless of late as the West's tendrils now reach beyond individual nations: the development and growth of multi-national corporations now make nation-states—their laws, religions, cultures, etcetera—much less significant than they were in the heyday of modern tramp literature just over a century ago, when vagabondage was still an option for those who wished to free themselves from the physical and mental straightjacket of mainstream society.

Four events in North America (which had by now joined European colonizers as a driving force behind the expansion of Western influence in the world) were responsible for a renaissance in vagabondage within its own borders: 1/ the end of the American Civil War in which thousands of former soldiers, well used to an outdoor life and tramping, found themselves homeless and ill-prepared for the domestic responsibilities of civilian life; 2/ the opening of the first transcontinental railroad in 1869; 3/ the first of a series of catastrophic international financial crashes and associated "depressions" (1873, 1893 and 1930), and, paradoxically, 4/ the gold-rushes of California (1848–1855) and 'Klondike' (the 1890s). It is not surprising then that, through choice or necessity, large numbers were thrown into a transient life, forced to roam the continent, surviving on whatever resources came to hand. A few of these chose the tramping lifestyle from a sense of moral purpose and a rejection of wider society's morality which they found difficult to reconcile with. They created their own sense of a 'republic', one not restricted to a geographical place, an ethnic group, religious or cultural traditions. Their's was a republic without boundaries or social distinctions who, like their ancient Greek Cynic forbears, regarded themselves as 'citizens of the world', free to roam wherever they felt the fancy, and adopting any customs and habits that suited their needs.

And yet, after a tradition spanning two and a half millennia from the birth of Western Civilization to recent times, tramping as an accepted—if not maligned—tradition, has all but been driven out of existence. As Jack Kerouac (1960, pp. 60–61) observed, vagabondage was already being outlawed and suppressed through the implementation of tougher vagrancy laws backed up by intensive police surveillance, including the use of helicopters, which meant that "you can't even be alone anymore in the primitive wilderness":

> In America camping is considered a healthy sport for Boy Scouts but a crime for mature men who have made it their vocation.—Poverty is considered a virtue among the monks of civilized nations—in America you spend a night in the calaboose if youre [sic] caught short without your vagrancy change. ... they pick on lovers on the beach even. they just dont [sic] know what to do with themselves in those five thousand dollar police cars with the two-way dick tracy radios except pick on anything that moves in the night and in the daytime on anything that seems to be moving independently of gasoline ...

And so, in some respect, the phenomena of vagabondage described in the pages that follow no longer exists. To remain under the radar today with the ubiquitous CCTV and electronic databases that analyze even our shopping habits, to exist without money, a registered address or ID, requires no little skill and has succeeded in eradicating most of the vagabond tradition in a way that various vagrancy acts failed to achieve. Having acknowledged all of this, in his book *Drift; Illicit Mobility and Uncertain Knowledge* (2018), Jeff Ferrell has brought to my attention a new subculture of young North American 'train hoppers' or 'gutter punks' (as they are described), with whom he spent some time. Their lifestyle has many parallels with the vagabonds writers cited in this text, including the methods of beating trains, yet it contains its own unique features, including "dishevelled black clothes and matted hair" and a deliberate gender ambiguity in which it is impossible to tell a girl from a boy on first encounter:

> Gutter punks' cultural inversion of cleanliness and filth, their conversion of ragged and dirty into ragged and right, is no abstract exercise. Instead, they construct this transformation from what's available and not available, from the day-to-day interplay of necessity, creativity and symbolic display. Like their tattoos, like their intertwined endeavours of train hopping, Dumpster diving, and flying a sign, dark clothes and dirt form a homologous relationship. Black clothes display subcultural identities while helping to hide members of the subculture from those who would apprehend them. (Ferrell, 2018, p. 131)

This newer cultural phenomenon requires its own research, and I could not possibly add anything to what Ferrell has experienced and written about in detail, including citations from the documentary film *Train on the Brain* (Murray, 2000) and a text about a similar phenomenon in Europe, *Off the Map*, (Chickena and Kat, 2003)—both accounts written by women.

Of course, other new forms of vagabondage are very much in evidence, particularly the virtual vagabonds and digital nomads who now inhabit cyberspace for similar reasons that those cited in this volume took to the open road. But they replace walking for knowledge and excitement, with surfing the world from a chair through a screen, a phenomenon that deserves greater attention in another book. Homelessness (which is often confused with vagabondage) and refugeeism may both also be on the increase of late, but these are not vagabondage in the sense of a deliberate lifestyle choice in close association with the natural world—to suggest such would be absurd.

A HISTORY OF VAGABOND PHILOSOPHY

But to return to the birth of Western Civilisation. The original philosophical battle that would define it—and continues to the present day—was waged at the time between the Hellenistic philosophers (Cynics, Hedonists, Stoics, Skeptics, Epicureans, etcetera) who, more akin to Eastern philosophies, believed that knowledge was relative and should be gained through our own sensory experiences, against those like Plato and Aristotle who believed that knowledge existed through first principles; pre-existing truths they held to apply universally, regardless of individual interpretation (Sharples, 1996, p. 11). And it is the latter, the Platonic, rationalist view of the world, that prevailed and has defined and dominated Western civilization for the past two and a half millennia, supported and frequently corrupted by scientists, academics, the judiciary, industrialists, politicians, indeed all those who define what Western society should be, and benefit disproportionally from its regulations and decrees. This is not, of course, to suggest that other human civilizations and cultures are any less corrupt or even responsible for tyrannical acts committed in their name— but this is a book about Western vagabonds, even if many subsequently turned their backs on the laws, traditions and boundaries imposed by their inherited cultures and adopted the entire planet as their natural home.

What is surprising, perhaps, is that this vagabond tradition and its opposition to many prevailing features of Western culture can be traced back to the very time that these cultural values were first being established. One does not have to research deeply to locate the contempt with which the Cynics, in particular, regarded Plato and Aristotle. And it is the Cynics' beliefs and behaviors that open this book because of evidence that the Cynics were the first representatives of a vagabond movement in opposition to Western culture. In Plato's writings, the Cynic Antisthenes (c. 446–366 BCE—a contemporary and friend of Socrates) found everything he felt adversely afflicted humanity: pride, falsehood, pretentiousness, arrogance, mystification, superstitious and religious humbug, the worship of the state, contempt towards what is concrete, and the misuse of language for the purpose of hiding one's own confusion (Navia, 1996, pp. 58-59). A simple anecdote on the classic Western obsession with categorizing everything—together with the Cynic's style of comedic satire—serves well to highlight the Cynics' scorn: when, in one of his lectures, Plato defined humans as "featherless bipeds," the Cynic, Diogenes of Sinope (c. 404–323 B.C.E.), returned with a plucked cockerel announcing, "This is Plato's man" (Laërtius, 1995, p. 231).

In such a manner, Plato frequently found himself on the receiving end of the Cynics' wrath for selling out to Socrates (Navia, 1996, p. 10), in the same way that, over five hundred years later, would leaders of the Christian Church hijack and misrepresent the thoughts of another vagabond philosopher, Jesus of Nazareth (man or myth is of no relevance here—and of whom more later). The march of progress theories in the West, associated with the Platonic and Aristotelian legacy, and the belief in grand narratives explaining our existence and having power and control over our lives, have marginalized and delegitimized other belief systems for centuries. For instance, Western medicine, dominated as it is by treating the symptoms rather than the causes of illness, can often be responsible for new or escalating illness (iatrogenesis)[1] and has sidelined alternative, often more efficacious interventions, putting them beyond the reach of ordinary folk because they sit outside of legitimized, state-funded, control. But this is a subject exhaustively covered in the texts cited in the footnote. The point here is that this Western obsession with medical cures did not escape the Cynics' attention, as is noted from the 6th Oration of Dio Chrysostom (cited in Dobbin, 2012, p. 96):

> Humans, by contrast [to the beasts, who drank only water, ate uncultivated plants and "were strong and healthy without the need for doctors"], clung desperately to life by resorting to various means of cheating death; and all the same few managed to reach old age. They lived with a host of complaints the majority of which don't even have a name. Since earth does not produce medicinal plants to cure them all, they are forced to submit to the cautery and the knife.

As will become clearer in the following chapters, it is not so much the vagabond philosopher's knowledge that the institutions of Western civilization are maintained by an egotistical drive for celebrity and success (defined as money, influence, power, etc.), it is more than the rest of humanity, Nietzsche's 'human herd', still believe that their civilization is something worthy of praise to be emulated by the rest of the globe. This cutting oneself off from the fundamental values of the society in which one lives leaves the vagabond on the horns of a dilemma, one which the contemporary German philosopher Peter Sloterdijk (1988, p. 119) refers to as "inner emigration": the choice between, "Get out or collaborate? Flee or stand firm?" Yet the true vagabond must have a natural wisdom in the first place that separates them from those who accept the human world as it has been developed by the civilizing processes. As Denis Diderot (who had to flee on publication of his first book and was pursued by French Government authorities to "suffer a punishment

---

[1] The evidence for which can be found in the numerous texts on iatrogenesis written over the past 50 years; from Ivan Illich's *Limits to Medicine: Medical Nemesis—The Expropriation of Health*, (1975), to Gabor Maté's *The Myth of Normal: Illness, health & healing in a toxic culture* (2023).

whose example will terrify [his] peers") reminded us anonymously in 1746, "The wise man sees far into the immense depth of possibilities; the idiot fails to imagine any possibilities outside of what already is" (Diderot, 2018, para. XXXII). This aspect of vagabondage: the manner in which the vagabond is philosophically and sometimes physically separated from their fellows, will be discussed further in the chapter titled, 'The Lone and Lofty Perch of World Hating Introspection', but it is also here worth noting the following observation from the Roman emperor Julian (331–363 CE), who rejected Christianity and promoted Cynicism, when he refers to the Cynics looking down at the mass of men from Mount Olympus: "Wandering blind in the valley of confusion" (cited in Dobbin, 2012, p. 201).

CYNICISM

As the claim is made here that Cynicism is essential to a proper understanding of the themes of modern vagabond literature (many writers of which refer directly to cynicism in both its ancient and modern meanings), I have included the following summary from my book, *Cynicism from Diogenes to Dilbert* (2005), and ask the reader to hold this description of the Cynic in their mind when considering the modern vagabond writer in the discussions that follow. The only aspect of Cynicism I suggest is *not* shared by most modern vagabond writers, was the Cynic's more public role as a 'performance artist', the deliberate strategy of shocking their 'audience' into a reevaluation of what the Cynic believed to be human beings false values. But then, not all Cynics engaged in these public 'performances' or saw it as their role to save other humans from their folly, and it is also clear that many modern vagabond writers clearly *did* see this as their role. However, for most of the writers and thinkers discussed in this book, their's was predominantly a personal philosophy for surviving in what they regarded as a hostile world of lies and manipulations. Neither, as previously emphasized, has the vagabond any interest in converting others to their way of life—theirs is not an evangelical creed. But here is a brief portrait of the Cynic:

> He or she would have worn similar attire, probably a simple cloak; any meagre possessions being carried in a small bag or wallet. We also know, that in spite of their close association with nature and their view that city life was unnatural, they would curiously almost always be seen in urban surroundings. The Cynic had no loyalty to family or state and rejected what they considered to be false values, adopting any customs which complemented their lifestyle. They considered themselves citizens of the world, or cosmos: the first cosmopolitans. The Cynic's ability to move around freely was further assisted by their resistance to being

owned by possessions. They had no interest in trying to convert others to their way of life, but welcomed anyone, regardless of social background, gender, or race to join their ranks. Whatever teaching a Cynic undertook was likely to be performed in public, sometimes in an irreverent or shocking manner, and if a Cynic did something, it was because they wanted to do it, not because they were compelled to do it. Diogenes in particular, reminded us that in spite of our pretensions as civilized beings, a denial of our animality was a repudiation of our true nature. An understanding of which, required focussing exclusively on the physical world in which we live, and abandoning supernatural and metaphysical beliefs (particularly religious faiths) which could only lead to disillusionment. The Cynic would not, therefore, defer happiness but live each day as though tomorrow might never arrive. Life, in any case did not follow a progression toward enlightenment but a cyclical series of mundane repetitions punctuated by occasional highs and lows. The Cynic did not believe in fortune or pre-destiny, rather striving to be masters of their own destiny. Askesis and ponos were the means by which the Cynic could achieve self-sufficiency and the indifference necessary to cope with all eventualities. If Cynicism was a philosophy at all, it was a practical one, aimed at training for a harsh life which was the Cynics expectation. And finally, their mission—certainly Diogenes'—was to deface the currency of human beings' false values and customs and thus discredit the fabrication that was civilized society. (Cutler, 2005, pp. 43-44)

More specific references to the Cynics will be made in the relevant chapters that follow, but first, below are listed some styles of discourse attributable to the Cynics because of their obvious influence—directly or indirectly—on modern vagabond literature, and also Biblical literary styles as will be acknowledged later in this Introduction.

CYNIC GENRES AND DISCOURSE

Diatribe

The diatribe is a written or verbal monologue, often addressed to an imaginary adversary as a forceful and bitter attack. It is an exposition rather than an argument, as there is only room for one speaker (Dudley,1937, p. 111). The Cynic Bion of Borysthenes (c. 325–250 BCE) is credited with its invention, yet examples of the diatribe (with powerful Cynic sentiments) can be found among pre-Socratic philosophers such as Heracles (c500 BCE), demonstrating that Cynic influences were certainly present before Cynicism formally coalesced as a movement:

> What do you think, you men? If God did not make dogs or sheep slaves, nor asses nor horses nor mules, did he then make men slaves? ... They do not reduce one another to slavery, nor does one eagle buy another eagle, nor does one lion pour wine for another lion, nor does one dog castrate another dog, ... Or how can you act piously toward a statue, when you have acted impiously against nature? (Heracles cited in Malherbe, 1977, p. 213)

Fragments of two diatribes from tramp writer Trader Horn, one cited below in this Introduction (also on the subject of slavery two and a half thousand years after Heracles), the other in Chapter 1, serve to illustrate the energy and biting sarcasm behind the diatribe. The diatribe is also credited as the prototype for the Christian sermon (Bakhtin, 1999, p. 12), even though Horn's second diatribe ridicules that religion.

Chreia

The *chreia* (literal meaning of which is 'something useful') accounts for most of the Diogenes stories and is a form of aphorism consisting of a comedic and ridiculing remark in response to a statement or situation (Sayre, 1938, p. 103). An example serves best to describe it. When asked if he believed in the gods, Diogenes replied, "How can I help believing in them, when I see a god-forsaken wretch like you?" (Laërtius, 1995, p. 45). On being reproached for eating in the market place (convention at the time forbade eating in public), "Well, it was in the market-place that I felt hungry" (Laërtius, 1995, p. 45). On being asked what wine he enjoyed drinking, Diogenes responded, "That which belongs to someone else" (Sayre, 1938, p. 103). And in a *chreia* credited to Antisthenes, on it being confirmed to him by a priest that initiates into the Orphic Mysteries enjoyed certain advantages in the after-life, Antisthenes replied, "Why then, don't you die!" (Laërtius, 1995, p. 5)

Soliloquy

Most associated today with Shakespeare's dramas ("To be, or not to be," "Is this a dagger which I see before me," etcetera), this style of discourse is credited to Antisthenes and is featured by 'thinking aloud,' the ability to conduct a conversation with oneself which allows the audience into the innermost thoughts of the speaker.

Parody

The Cynic Crates (c. 365—c. 285 BCE) has been credited with establishing this satirical device as a tool for defacing traditional beliefs and values by comic imitations of them to enhance their absurdity. Crates pupil, Menippus of Gadar, further developed parody in his own brand of satire described below (Branham, 1996, p. 10-11). The following is an example of the genre (from a longer piece) used by the modern tramp writer Morley Roberts who, admitting he has no learned degree, ridicules formal education by setting a mock examination paper which he says, "might appal many fat graduates" and yet is clearly one that Roberts would pass with distinction:

1. Describe from experience the sensations of hunger when prolonged over three days.

2. Explain the differences in living in New York, Chicago and San Francisco on a dollar a week. In such cases, how would you spend ten cents if you found it in the street at three o'clock in the morning?

3. How long would it be in your own case before want of food destroyed your sense of private property? Give examples from your own experience.

4. How far can you walk without food—(a) when you are trying to reach a definite point; (b) when you are walking with an insane view of getting to some place unknown where a good job awaits you?

5. If, after a period (say three weeks) of moderate starvation and two days of absolute starvation, you are offered some work, which would be considered laborious by the most energetic coal-heaver, would you tackle it without food or risk the loss of the job by requesting your employer to advance you 15 cents for breakfast?

6. Can you admire mountain scenery—(a) when you are very hungry; (b) when you are very thirsty? If you have any knowledge of the ascetic ecstasy, describe the symptoms.

7. You are in South-west Texas without money and without friends. How would you get to Chicago in a fortnight? What is

the usual procedure when a town objects to impecunious tramps staying around more than twenty-four hours? Can you describe a "calaboose"?

8. Sketch an American policeman. Is he equally polite to a railroad magnate and a tramp? What do you understand by 'fanning with a club'?

(Roberts, 1904, pp. 57-59)

Menippean Satire

The *menippea* is the most influential and enduring of all Cynic genres, as all of those styles already discussed above have been absorbed into it. Its style involves caricaturing pseudo-intellectual fraud by interjecting the actual words of learned sages of the time into parodies, then satirizing them with incongruous verses, songs, curses, etcetera, to push their logic to absurd extremes and amplify the ridicule (Rose, 1993, pp. 85-86). With its roots in carnivalized folklore (see below), Mennipus' work is better known today through its imitations by other cynics, and also classical writers such as Varro, Lucian and Seneca (Navia, 1992, p. 182). A modern example of the genre can be found in William Blake's *The Marriage of Heaven and Hell* in which Blake deliberately reverses notions of good and evil in order to shock the reader into rethinking conventionally held beliefs. Menippus is also famous for his satirical laughter, referred to by Lucian as "the secret dog who bites as he laughs," even following the dead into Hades to continue his mockery (Navia, 1992, p. 182).

Symposium

Although not a cynic invention, the symposium has strong links with other Cynic genres because of its origins in the Socratic and the carnivalesque. Described as a banquet dialogue (Bakhtin, 1999, p. 120), the informal setting of the symposium—no doubt eased by food and wine—creates an ambiance of familiarity, frankness, and eccentricity. What marks the Cynics' use of the symposium is that, unlike the Greek convention of the time in which the symposium was open only to men, and then of a certain standing in society, the Cynics welcomed women to join the revelry as equals. Diogenes Laërtius (author of *Lives and Opinions of Eminent Philosophers*—third century CE—not to be confused with Diogenes of Sinope) relates a story of Hipparchia (c. 325 BCE), wife of Crates, accompanying him to such a banquet where she challenges the atheist Theodorus to a verbal and physical duel, the description of which identifies the Cynic acceptance of women as philosophical equals (Laërtius, 1995, 6:97). For further evidence of the Cynics' attitude towards women, below is an excerpt from Crates' 29th letter to his wife in which he uses the term "female liberation," and a further reference to slavery:

> ... we bravely defy pain and popular opinion when most people can't. That is the real reason why the label 'dog' was first attached to us [the Cynics]. You are no weaker by nature, any more than bitches are weaker than male dogs. Female liberation will then be justified on grounds of nature, since it is acknowledged that slavery in general, if not based on proven inferiority, exists by mere convention. (cited in Dobbin, 2012, p. 70)

Claims that Mary Magdalene might have shared such a meal with Jesus and his disciples at The Last Supper might be part of modern myth-making and mischief on the part of Leonardo Da Vinci, but it would fit with the Cynic influence on Jesus discussed further below.

Carnival

Likewise not a Cynic invention, but because certain aspects of carnival had an influence on Cynic styles of discourse, it is worth briefly discussing what its main elements were. The main feature of the carnival, picked up by Menippus, was the reversal of normal positions in society, for example, the fool or clown dominating the proceedings. In carnival mode, one could mock the king or queen and ridicule and pour profanities on other public figures and deities, behavior that may have resulted in death outside of the protective bubble of the carnival tradition. Whether it was one's essential way of life or a way of letting of steam on festive occasions, the outcome of both Cynicism and carnival was to suspend the laws, prohibitions, and restrictions that determine the structure of 'civilized', mannered society. For the brief duration of the carnival, this had the levelling effect of freeing people from socio-hierarchical positions of rank, age, property, etcetera, and liberating them from the normal restraints and restrictions of society—something the Cynics and modern vagabonds adopted as a permanent way of life.

A note on the Cynic genres: in his book *Problems of Dostoevesky's Poetics*, Mikhail Bakhtin (1999, p. 113) describes all of the Cynic genres discussed above under the generic term *serio-comical*. The seriocomic genres of ancient Greece are united by their opposition to what Bakhtin (1999, p. 81) describes as the monological serious genres (viz. Plato, Aristotle, et al.): those that involve a "pedagogical discourse," whereby "someone who knows and possesses the truth instructs someone who is ignorant of it"—the very discourse that the Cynics were compelled to ridicule.

JESUS OF NAZARETH: SON OF GOD OR VAGABOND PHILOSOPHER?

The most independent reference of the time to the existence of a historical Jesus is said to come from the writings of Roman/Jewish historian Flavius Josephus, but as Josephus was not born until around four years after Jesus was reportedly crucified, his accounts are not contemporaneous. Neither are those of the Roman historian Tacitus, who, while recording the same facts as Josephus about Jesus' crucifixion, published his account about 20 years after Josephus' work. However, as noted earlier, I am not concerned here with the argument as to whether Jesus was a historical or a mythical figure—or even a supernatural phenomenon. Given the immense authority still accorded to Christianity in the modern world, his original philosophy, so much as it can be identified, is relevant to the subject under discussion here.

Many claims have been made (on the surface bizarre) as to Jesus' identity, such as Jesus the magician (Morton Smith) or Jesus the first stand-up Jewish comic (Robert Funk), but for the purposes of this book, I claim Jesus as a vagabond philosopher and provide below some evidence to support that characterization. This includes similar claims from modern vagabond writers themselves, those who were clearly drawn to Jesus' lifestyle and philosophy as presented by some New Testament writers. As most of these accounts were semi-fictional, it is hardly surprising that there are conflicting interpretations of his life and teachings—suiting those who have the right to choose. I do not suggest that the lifestyle of Jesus (any more than that of the Cynics) is comparable to that of nineteenth and twentieth-century vagabonds who lived in a very different world, not least the availability of freight-trains and the necessity to travel vast distances in search of work or adventure—even though Jesus did advocate discarding home and family ties; nor is there any evidence that Jesus was afflicted by wanderlust as presented in this text, but there was certainly much of his character for the modern day vagabond to identify with and to regard him as part of their fraternity.

But firstly, what is the evidence that Jesus' lifestyle and philosophy may have been influenced by the Cynics. Even committed Christians, such as the Anglian priest F. Gerald Downing in his *Christians and Cynic Origins*, have concluded that ancient Greek Cynicism was the most likely model for Jesus' ascetic lifestyle and aphoristic wisdom sayings (Downing, 1992, p. 302). And, as Robert Dobbin (2012, p. xxxviii) points out in his translation of the writings of Cynic philosophers, "first-century Galilee was a world in which Hellenistic ideas collided with Jewish thought and tradition." So, in terms of Jesus' lifestyle, his philosophy, his style of discourse, his asceticism, his attitude toward others, and his troublesome behavior, what were the opportunities for Jesus to have met with and been influenced by Cynics?

The main trade route between the Mediterranean coastal town of Ptolemais (present-day Acre) and Gadara (birthplace of Cynics Menippus, Meleager and Oenomaus) near the south-eastern end of the Sea of Galilee passed just 8 miles north of Nazareth and even closer to Sepphoris (Herod Antipas' governmental seat and the largest city in Galilee during Jesus' lifetime). Although there is no specific mention of Jesus ever having visited Sepphoris, it is unlikely that he would not have come into contact with Cynics from this city, located only five miles from Nazareth. Even more unlikely, is that Nazareth and neighboring communities would not have been influenced by the dominance of their important Hellenized neighbor. Even so, the first recorded contact between a named Cynic and Christians is not reported until the second century by the Syrian satirist Lucian of Samosata (c. 120-190 CE) in his *The Passing of Peregrinus* (1996). Lucian actually witnessed Peregrinus' dramatic suicide at the Olympic Games of 165 CE when Peregrinus, having publicized the event in advance, threw himself onto his own funeral pyre in front of admiring Cynics and a bemused general public alike. Peregrinus seems to have been one of those rare individuals for whom it seemed possible to reconcile being both a Cynic and a Christian.

Likewise, the earliest comparison between Christians and Cynics comes from the second-century anti-Christian Greek philosopher Celsus (175–177 CE), who made disparaging comparisons about Christians' Cynic-like behaviour of preaching to the rabble in the market place rather than engaging in what he considered intelligent debate; a view challenged by Origen some 60 years later when he commended the practice of bringing philosophy to the mass of uneducated people (Downing, 1992, p. 21). Hence, Cynicism is described as a philosophy of the proletariat and also of the individual. Christian and Cynic street preachers would likely have shared the same audiences.

But back to the style of discourse itself; regardless of the actual message, the style and delivery of both early Christian and Cynic public speaking was based on the same modes of discourse. As acknowledged earlier, the Cynic diatribe was the prototype for the Christian sermon, and the aphoristic sayings of early Christian texts are often indistinguishable from the Cynic *chreia*. For instance, when asked why his disciples did not wash their hands before eating, Jesus replies, "You hypocrites! . . . [it is] not what goes into the mouth defiles a man, but what comes out of the mouth, this defiles a man" (Matthew 15.1-11). And in a typical example of the *chreia* in the non-canonical gospel of Thomas

(Ehrman, 2003, verse 53), when asked by his disciples if circumcision was beneficial or not, Jesus responds, "If it were beneficial, their father would beget them already circumcised from their mother." The contempt Jesus shows for Jewish laws and practices has direct parallels with the Cynics' contempt for Athenian laws and practices, as also does Jesus' asceticism. This included instructions not to worry about what one eats, to discard home and family ties, to eschew normal standards of cleanliness, and to treasure ourselves rather than our possessions: "Go sell all your possessions and give them to the poor" (Mark 10:21); "Don't take anything on your journey except a stick" (Mark 6:8); "It is easier for a camel to go through the eye of a needle than for a rich man to enter the kingdom of God" (Mark 10:25). Compare also, the truism in 1 Timothy (6.10) that, "the love of money is the root of all evils," with that attributed to Diogenes in Laërtius (6:50), "the love of money is the mother-city of all evils." What remains a mystery, given what is written in the Gospels about Jesus' teachings, is how Christianity survived as the banner of Western civilization and the degree to which Christians have forgotten Jesus' mortal, tramping beginnings. His vagabond philosophy has certainly not been practiced by most self-professed Christians for centuries, indeed, the religion as practiced by most of its adherents represents everything the vagabond seeks to exile him or herself from. As I noted in an earlier essay:

> The image of fat bishops in their cathedral palaces, clad in purple robes and gold chains, just does not sit comfortably with Jesus the ascetic sage entreating his followers to abandon money, possessions and a roof over their head for a life of hardship and prayer. (Cutler, 2010, p. 373)

To finish this section, it is worth noting how the literal acceptance of Biblical 'truths' may be reconsidered to get closer to the philosophy of the Cynics. For instance, the 'Kingdom of God' could be viewed as no more than a philosophical attitude that would allow one to transcend the narrow cultural divides, petty rules and artificial taboos of earthly kingdoms. In this sense, kingship becomes a metaphor for the sovereignty of spirit and self-control in which the independent, superior person could rule their own life. And in terms of the concept of 'heaven,' a line exists in the second-century Epistle of Mathetes to Diognetus that could be equally applied to the Cynics, it notes that, "Christians sojourn among things domed to corruption . . . [and] under daily punishment flourish all the more" (Bettenson, 1990, pp. 54-55). The following passage from the same epistle proposes a concept of 'heaven' that exactly matches Cynic cosmopolitanism:

> They [Christians] live in countries of their own, but as sojourners. They share all things as citizens; they suffer all things as foreigners. Every

foreign land is their native place, every native place is foreign. . . . They pass their life on earth; but they are citizens in heaven. (Bettenson, 1990, pp. 54-55)

This view, that heaven could be an attitude of the living rather than a repository for dead souls, is borne out by Jesus himself as reported in Thomas (113): when asked by his disciples, "When will the kingdom come?" Jesus answers, "It will not come by waiting for it. It will not be a matter of saying 'here it is' or 'there it is.' Rather, the kingdom of the father is spread out upon the earth, and men do not see it." That one could live the right life now here on earth, not through the deferred gratification of an afterlife, is also confirmed in Luke (17:20-21) who reports that on being asked when the kingdom of God would come, Jesus replies, it is not a place or a thing, it is "in the midst of" or within those who believe in it.

A NOTE ON NIETZSCHE'S DIATRIBE ON CHRISTIANITY—AND THAT OF TRAMP WRITERS ALSO

At the same time that hobos were being persecuted across America, Friedrich Nietzsche was writing in Germany about the hypocrisy between what Jesus originally stood for and the mischief carried out in his name—carried along under the banner of improving and enlightening people. Like Jesus, Nietzsche's thoughts have been claimed for many different causes, including fascism, and he has also been in and out of fashion depending on the cultural prejudices of those who write about him. While Nietzsche's writings can be contradictory at times, for my own part, I read them as consistent and highly insightful on the central themes of this book. Neither do I have a problem with Nietsche's apparent self-aggrandizement, which provides power and authority to views that were very challenging to the prevailing ones of his day. I personally find them both refreshing and humorous. For Nietzsche, rather than egotistical posturing, they reinforce his concern that humans had become too slavish to prevailing dogma and should think for themselves.

Son and grandson of Lutheran ministers, Nietzsche may have been 'Anti-Christ' (the title of his 13th book), but, as his sister Elizabeth acknowledges, he had "a tender love for the founder of Christianity" (referring, of course, to Jesus, not Paul). What incensed Nietzsche was the way that Paul had transformed Jesus into the Christ figure in order to promote his own perverted brand of religion. For Nietzsche, the whole history of Christianity, from the death on the cross onward, is the history of a misunderstanding of an original symbolism, replaced by a hostility to all of the great values of the past (Nietzsche, 1999, p. 54).

> The figure of the Saviour, his teaching, his way of life, his death, the meaning of his death, even the consequences of his death—nothing remained untouched, nothing remained in even remote contact with reality. Paul simply shifted the centre of gravity of that whole life to behind this existence in the lie of the 'risen' Jesus. (Nietzsche, 1999, p. 60)

As for Nietzsche's own credentials as a modern Cynic philosopher (if not a modest one), these can be found throughout his writings. From *Ecce Homo*: "There is altogether no prouder and at the same time more exquisite kind of book than my books—they attain here and there the highest thing that can be attained on earth, cynicism." (Nietzsche, 1992, p. 43)

And from *Beyond Good and Evil*:

> Cynicism is the only form in which base souls approach what is called honesty; and the higher man must open his ears to all the coarser or finer cynicism and congratulate himself when the clown becomes shameless right before him, or the scientific satyr speaks out. (Nietzsche, 1909, p. 39)

Nietzsche sought his contentment in the Cynic sense of living an ascetic lifestyle on his meager pension, a lifestyle which outwardly exhibited itself as very simple, embracing the minimum necessary for life as a strategy for survival. His total abstinence from alcohol was a denial which even Diogenes did not endure, and the tiny room where he lived and worked, devoid of decoration or comfort, has parallels with Diogenes' own choice of dwelling:

> There is no doubt that . . . my brother tried a little bit to imitate Diogenes in the tub; he wanted to find out with how little could a philosopher do.
>
> (Elizabeth Forster-Nietzsche cited by Niehues-Probsting in Branham & Goulet-Caze, 1996, p. 359)

> Indeed, a minimum of life, an unchaining from all coarser desires, an independence in the middle of all kinds of outer nuisance; a bit of Cynicism, perhaps a bit of 'tub'.
>
> (Nietzsche cited by Niehues-Probsting in Branham & Goulet-Caze, 1996, p. 359)

Nietzsche's sentiments on Jesus are shared by tramp writers discussed in my earlier writing, many of whom adopted the Galilean as a fellow vagabond philosopher. For example, Thomas Manning Page described Jesus as the ultimate leader of an itinerant tramp movement (Cutler, 2020, p.7), and Jim Tully, although admitting to never having believed in God or the living Christ, yet acknowledges a soft spot for Jesus in the role of a fictional tramp activist (Cutler, 2020, p.71). From Bart Kennedy's first prison sentence, he describes the pleasure he got from attending the prison chapel, not because he was religious but because he sought inspiration from Jesus as a fellow tramp and lawbreaker who would have identified with his situation: "The Man whose name would live while the world lasted had been a tramp and a criminal" (Kennedy, 1900, p. 137). Kennedy also observed that the corruption of Jesus by Christians, means that if one such as Jesus were to appear in our city center streets today, he would be rejected and treated just as any other tramp. Stephen Graham well understood the corrupting influence of the New Testament and leaves us in no doubt as to which version of Christianity sustained him in his tramping:

> the cultured would disdain it, until a new St. Paul interpreted it for them in terms that they could understand, so giving it a 'vogue.' Both the peasants and the cultured would be christians, but with this difference, that in one case the seed would be growing on the surface, and in the other from the depths. The peasant, of course, has no surface; he is the good black earth all ready for the seed. (Graham, 1913, p. 304)

And from Trader Horn's diatribe on slavery (1932, pp. 159–163) in which he criticizes British parliamentarians' hypocrisy for turning a blind eye to the practice, in spite of their Christian pretensions, he comments:

> What'd Christ do in the circumstances? ... did He ever cover up His eyes from wickedness and fall back on prayer? ... doesn't Jesus Himself forbid slavery? "Feed my sheep" and so on ... What's become of His teaching? Where are the apostles of Jesus to-day? nothing but homo stultus [human stupidity] if slavery's still rife after two thousand years.

Kennedy's reference to Jesus as a fellow criminal seems, on the face of it, an outrageous proposition, but it helps focus the debate about what criminality actually means in the West. The stories as handed down do not dispute that Jesus was executed for treason and blasphemy; so by this definition, Jesus clearly *was* a criminal, but, herein lies the central debate regarding Plato's belief in first principles versus the relativism of the Hellenic philosophers, the concept of criminality depends on the legitimacy of the laws that define it. There is no need to look further than the reversal of United States abortion laws in 2022 to answer this question. In this case, whether a woman having an abortion is a criminal act or not depends solely on which political party is in government and which Supreme Court judges they elect. If the political party is a conservative one dominated by a belief in orthodox Christian dogma, they will elect conservative Christian judges. And so the most powerful and influential so-called 'democracy' in the West is yet able to criminalize its citizens because those in power at the time believed abortion to be criminal. But the following quotation from Henry Thoreau (1911, p. 94) captures the relativity of 'the law' and a true vagabond's response to it, much more eloquently than I can:

> There is something servile in the habit of seeking after a law which we may obey. We may study the laws of matter at and for our convenience, but a successful life knows no law. It is an unfortunate discovery certainly, that of a law which binds us where we did not know before that we were bound. Live free, child of the mist,—and with respect to knowledge we are all children of the mist. The man who takes the liberty to live is superior to all the laws, by virtue of his relation to the lawmaker.

To complete the circle then between Nietzsche, the Cynics, Christianity and the birth of Western Civilization, the following passage from Nietzsche's work *Twilight of the Idols: or, how to philosophize with a hammer* (1997, p. 87) concisely summarizes the connections when he laments the loss of the Hellenistic philosophies and denounces Plato's influence on Western culture (which he detested almost as much as St. Paul's):

> Plato is boring.—Ultimately, my mistrust of Plato reaches into the depths; I find him so divergent from all the fundamental instincts of the Hellenes, so over moralized, such a Christian before his time . . . how much Plato there still is in the concept "Church", in the structure, system, and practice of the Church.

But the final words on Christianity and its incompatibility with the natural world, I leave to Denis Diderot (2018, paragraphs 111, V, and XXI), who, over 100 years before Nietzsche, cut straight to the absurdity of the matter with his own blunt and unarguable logic:

> "Why harass me by miracles, when all it takes to floor me is a syllogism? What then—could it actually be easier to heal the lame than to enlighten me?"

> "If God, who gave us the gift of reason, also demands that we sacrifice it, then he's a swindler who steals back what he gave you."

"If reason is a gift from Heaven, and if the same can be said of faith, then Heaven has given us a pair of incompatible and contradictory gifts."

"To escape this impasse, we must say that faith is an illusory principle, and that it does not exist in nature."

"To prove the Gospel by means of a miracle is to prove an absurdity by something that is against nature."

Having provided a history of vagabondage, and emphasized what this book does *not* cover, the reader will now be introduced to the following features that are common to ancient and modern vagabond writers alike—principally through an examination of their own writing: Chapter 1 explores the enigma that is wanderlust, both as a compulsive urge to be on the move, and as a curse that its victims cannot resist; Chapter 2 looks at the vagabonds affinity with the nature, what they learn from lower animals and the tensions for them between the natural and the civilised worlds; In contrast, Chapter 3 discusses vagabondage in urban surroundings and associated practices such as bohemianism and *flânerie*; Chapter 4 covers the vagabond's alienation and cutting oneself off from the fundamental values of the society in which they live; Chapter 5 discusses the loss of childhood and advantages of 'ignorance' over the 'civilizing' process that strips the world of its magic; Chapter 6 discusses the blurring in vagabond writing—often intentionally—between autobiography and fiction, which although not unique to vagabond writers, was introduced to the reader a century and a half before 'autobiographical fiction' came back into vogue in the West as a new literary fad; and Chapter 7 combines all these features of vagabondage in an attempt to summarise what the principal features of this lifestyle and philosophy are.

Chapter 1

WANDERLUST

> What is this wanderlust? There's no way to define it, one just knows when one has it, or is afflicted by it. It is more than just wanting to go somewhere. Some might call it a form of neurosis, and maybe they're right. It may come upon you when you least expect it to. You don't need to have heard, as did Hank Williams, that lonesome whistle blow.
>
> Jim Christy (cited in Cutler, 2019, p. 322)

Former BBC TV presenter Bob Langley (1938—), a close contemporary of the modern vagabond cited above, provides his own take on wanderlust below. Having had to put off his dream of becoming a hobo, firstly on the death of his father and the need to support his mother, then on being called up for national service in the British armed forces at the age of 18, in 1959, at the age of 21, Langley took off to tramp America for three years, noting in his book *Lobo: A Vagabond in America* (1977, pp. 12-13) the following comments on wanderlust:

> I can think of no reason, no logical reason, that is, why I decided to go on the road, but from as far back as could remember, I had been filled with an unrest I could never explain, not even to myself. ... All through boyhood I had dreamed of escape, a secret dream, too ephemeral to put a voice to. I was obsessed with the idea of mobility. I spent weekends hitch-hiking up and down the countryside, sleeping in fields and barns and railway waiting rooms, but that was never, to my way of thinking, hobo-ing. Hobo-ing meant America. ... In the words of the Tom Paxton song, I was already a hobo in my mind, bumming rides, hopping freights, caught in the grip of migratory fever. I gobbled up the volumes of Kerouac and Jack London, listened to the songs of the open road, heard in my mind the clickety-clack of the boxcar frames and dreamed of hard travelling in a land I had never seen and could only begin to guess at.

Langley adds that from an early age, he had an equal compulsion to write, "an inextinguishable urge to communicate," but because his writing, "had not moved my teachers to expressions of awe and admiration," he concluded that he needed something to write about. "Hobo-ing would give me that experience."

The above two quotations from modern vagabonds capture the enigma that is 'wanderlust.' With the help of older vagabond writers cited throughout this text, I will attempt here to shed some further clarity on what it is to be smitten by this condition and why certain people are so smitten. But perhaps the first thing to acknowledge, as do Christy and Langley above, is that it arises from an irresistible and compulsive urge that true vagabonds find impossible to ignore. This need to be on the move, some endogenous drive toward 'foreign' experiences (real or imagined), is described by tramp writer Josiah Flynt (1908, p. 108) in his autobiography *My Life*, further identifying that, in his case, it was a stronger affliction in his youth:

> To-day I can laugh at all this, but it was a very serious matter in those days; unless I covered a certain number of miles each day or week, and saw so many different States, cities, rivers and kinds of people, I was disappointed—Hoboland was not giving me my share of her bounteous supply of fun and change. Of course, I was called "railroad crazy" by the quieter roadsters in whom the fever, as such, had long since subsided, but I did not mind. Farther, farther, farther! this was what I insisted on and got.

The phenomena of the child tramp or 'road kid' (a class of tramps of which he, together with tramp writers Livingstone, Everson, Davies, Kennedy, London, Horn, Tully, Phelan, and Christy, were all representatives) will be discussed further in the chapter titled 'The Peter Pan Syndrome', but staying with Josiah Flynt, from another of his books, *Tramping with Tramps* (1901, p. 53), we are given more on wanderlust as a compulsion, that urge to hit the road that comes in waves for no particular reason and must be obeyed, and also, that it can be a transitory affair:

> they [road kids] are possessed of the "railroad fever" ... the expression in its broader sense of Wanderlust. They want to get out into the world, and at stated periods the desire is so strong and the road so handy that they simply cannot resist the temptation to explore it. A few weeks usually suffice to cool their ardor, and then they run home quite as summarily as they left, but they stay only until the next runaway mood seizes them.

In his book *The Road*, Jack London, seven years Flynt's junior and heavily influenced by Flynt's writings (both would die prematurely from alcohol damage), refers to this same random and serendipitous nature of tramping described above:

> Perhaps the greatest charm of tramp-life is the absence of monotony. In Hobo Land the face of life is protean—an ever changing phantasmagoria, where the impossible happens and the unexpected jumps out of the bushes at every turn of the road. The hobo never knows what is going to happen the next moment; hence, he lives only in the present moment. He has learned the futility of telic endeavor, and knows the delight of drifting along with the whimsicalities of Chance. (London, 1907, pp. 85-86)

Christy acknowledged wanderlust as being "afflicted" by "a form of neurosis," Flynt as "railroad fever," and being described as "railroad crazy." This suggests wanderlust is some kind of curse, even if fuelled by positive desires for adventure. Arthur Rickett (1906, pp. 3-4) likens these combined emotions of pleasure-seeking and restlessness to some 'primal wildness' in the vagabond spirit:

> Restlessness, then, is one of the notes of the Vagabond temperament.
>
> Sometimes the Vagabond is a physical, sometimes only an intellectual wanderer; but in any case there is about him something of the primal wildness of the woods and hills.

THE PLEASURE OF WANDERLUST

> Oh the joy of walking! I've never felt it so strong in me ... the trance like, swimming, flying through the air; the current of sensations and ideas; and the slow, but fresh change of down, of road, of colour: all this churned up into a fine thin sheet of perfect calm happiness.
>
> Virginia Woolf (1982, p. 246)

> One of the pleasantest things is going on a journey; but I like to go by myself. . . . The soul of a journey is liberty, perfect liberty, to think, feel, do just as one pleases.
>
> William Hazlitt (1822)

To counter then, what some may take from the above discussion as wanderlust being a 'pathological condition,' a curse of tramp life, it is worth here looking more closely at the simple pleasures of the vagabond lifestyle. In the passage that follows, Rickett acknowledges both aspects of wanderlust: the "wild luxuriance" of the literary vagabond together with the inevitable "thorns and briars" that accompany vagabond life. Having wandered far from the beaten track, he says, the vagabond is able to bring back accounts that those of us who never stray far from home could not imagine:

> There is a wild luxuriance about his character that is interesting and fascinating ... The riotous growth of eccentricities and idiosyncrasies are picturesque enough, though you must expect to find thorns and briars. (Rickett, 1906, p. 111)

And in his chapter on Thomas de Quincey, Rickett describes the positive side of the literary vagabond's compulsion to wander (one shared equally by the tramp writer) as follows:

> He will follow any path that promises to be interesting, not so much with the scholar's patient investigation as with the pedestrian's delight in 'fresh woods and pastures new.' (Rickett, 1906, p. 47)

Harriet Martineau, although a scholar (credited as the first woman sociologist) and from a middle class background, and in spite of significant health problems, was herself a compulsive walker of significant achievements. In the passage below, she echoes the pleasures and the liberation of walking cited above and below. Strange, though, that she should use the masculine pronoun to describe "the pedestrian traveller", but that probably says more about publishers in 1800s than it does about the author:

> the wisest and happiest traveller is the pedestrian. ... There is no such freeman on earth as he is for the time. His amount of toil is usually within his own choice ... He can go on and stop when he likes: if a fit of indolence overtakes him, he can linger for a day or a week in any spot that pleases him. ... The pleasure is indescribable of saying to one's self, 'I will go there,'—'I will rest yonder,'—and forthwith accomplishing it. ... He is secure of his sleep, be his chamber ever so sordid ... Even the weather seems to be of less consequence to the pedestrian than to other travellers. (Martineau, 1838, pp. 53-54)

In the following passage from Robert Louis Stevenson's essay 'Walking Tours' (1876, pp. 685-690), that writer (although like Woolf and Hazlitt, a celebrity vagabond writer) distinguishes between the simple pleasures of the casual walker and pleasures experienced by those who are "of the brotherhood," true vagabond writers:

> It must not be imagined that a walking tour, as some would have us fancy, is merely a better or worse way of seeing the country. There are

many ways of seeing landscape quite as good; and none more vivid, in spite of canting dilettantes, than from a railway train. But landscape on a walking tour is quite accessory. He who is indeed of the brotherhood does not voyage in quest of the picturesque, but of certain jolly humours—of the hope and spirit with which the march begins at morning, and the peace and spiritual repletion of the evening's rest. He cannot tell whether he puts his knapsack on or takes it off with more delight. The excitement of the departure puts him in key for that of the arrival. Whatever he does will be further rewarded in the sequel; and so pleasure leads on to pleasure in an endless chain.

Charles Dickens (1905, eBook, no page numbers) also provided an account of the difference, for himself at least, between the walker and the vagabond:

My walking is of two kinds: one, straight on end to a definite goal at a round pace; one, objectless, loitering, and purely vagabond. In the latter state, no gipsy on earth is a greater vagabond than myself; it is so natural to me, and strong with me, that I think I must be the descendant, at no great distance, of some irreclaimable tramp.

To demonstrate that there is little difference in the way this joy of walking is expressed by the literary vagabond and the tramp writer, the following two passages describe how the pleasures of walking are linked to its health benefits. The first from W. H. Davies's book *The Autobiography of a Super-Tramp* (Davies, 2013, p. 166):

What a glorious time of the year is this! With the warm sun travelling through serene skies, the air clear and fresh above you, which instils new blood in the body, making one defiantly tramp the earth, kicking the snows aside in the scorn of action. The cheeks glow with health, the lips smile, and there is no careworn face seen, save they come out of the house of sickness of death.

The second is a description of Walt Whitman by Rickett (1906, p. 205):

He has spoken to us of 'the amplitude of the earth, and the coarseness and sexuality of the earth, and the great charity of the earth.' And he has done this with the rough outspokenness of the elements, with the splendid audacity of Nature herself. Brawn, sun-tan, air-sweetness are things well worth the having, for they mean good health. That is why we welcome the big, genial sanity of Walt Whitman, for he has about him the rankness and sweetness of the Earth.

Kathleen Phelan was perhaps the most prolific of the tramp writers in terms of responding to wanderlust, spending 77 of her 97 years on the road. Yet, in spite of the many dangers and discomforts she encountered as a tramp, she never considered an alternative way of living. Her second solo trip (following the death of her husband, tramp writer Jim Phelan) took three years in which she walked and hitchhiked, with her few possessions in a basket on wheels, through France, Spain, Morocco, Algeria, Tunisia, Libya, Egypt, Lebanon, Turkey, Iran, Iraq, Afghanistan, Pakistan, India, to Nepal, adding to her return journey, Kuwait, Cyprus, Greece, and Italy. Below, Kathleen Phelan (1972) describes her own attitude to wanderlust:

> Fine weather or foul I am out on the road. I own nothing but what I stand up in and can carry with me; I rarely have more than a couple of copper coins to rub together and yet you'd have to go far to find a happier woman.
>
> There is nothing to compare with the excitement of walking each day and never knowing who you are going to meet and where you are going to find yourself by nightfall.

Of course, one of the main pleasures the vagabond seeks to encounter on the road, no matter how many times they are drawn back for a spell of city life, is to get closer to nature, but this is the subject of the chapter that follows.

THE MOMENTUM OF TRAMPING

Another essential ingredient of wanderlust, acknowledged by Christy in the opening quotation, is that this urge to wander does not involve a planned destination. As I concluded in the final two sentences of my book on Christy, it is the need to be moving, not the destination, that fuels wanderlust, "This is tramping as a sheer life force. Without the constant onward movement the tramp is unable to breath and loses the reason for their existence" (Cutler, 2019, p. 327). All the writers cited in this Chapter allude to this fundamental element of wanderlust: that it is the momentum of tramping itself that pulls the tramp ever onward. As Blaise Cendrars (2004, p. 168) put it, "Keep going or drop dead! That is the order of the day, and 'depart' is the password of vagabonds." Although the tramp is occasionally forced to stop or rest, sometimes from exhaustion due to illness or disability, for respite and a bite to eat, or due to time in jail, the destination of the journey is always deferred. Such a condition is described below by Robert Louis Stevenson, firstly from *Travels with a Donkey in the Cevennes* (2022, p. 106) and secondly from *An Inland Voyage* (1904, p. 119):

> For my part, I travel not to go anywhere, but to go. I travel for travel's sake. The great affair is to move; to feel the needs and hitches of our life more nearly; to come down off this feather-bed of civilisation, and find the globe granite underfoot and strewn with cutting flints.
>
> And we must all set our pocket-watches by the clock of fate. There is a headlong, forthright tide, that bears away man with his fancies like a straw, and runs fast in time and space.

In Leslie Stephen's essay 'In Praise of Walking' (cited in Belloc, 1911, pp. 195-196), he expands further on this theme of moving with no fixed destination:

> Free from all bothers of railway time-tables and extraneous machinery, you trust to your own legs, stop when you please, diverge into any track that takes your fancy, and drop in upon some quaint variety of human life at every inn where you put up for the night.

In the fragment of a diatribe below from tramp writer Trader Horn's *Harold the Webbed* (1928, p. 213-214), this writer goes further than simply acknowledging this compulsion to be on the move, making the further case that, given the world created for us, *not* to submit to wanderlust is an absurdity:

> Doesn't the dawn come everyday calling you to move on? No camp should last forever. And that's where civilization makes the mistake of its life, trying to cage the natural man. Trying to make a stationary object behind bars. Did the great Onlooker give us the world plus the ocean to entice the thoughts of the roamer if he meant us to stay in one spot. ... All the luxuries of the haut ton are neither more or less than neck-irons to a slave. And what's worse they make heaven itself into the image of a cage. Why, the son of Mary Himself couldn't stand too much of the synagogue. ... Consider the lilies, he said. But the religioners've put no lilies in heaven.

But no one has perhaps captured the pure existential spirit of the momentum of wanderlust better than Leon Ray Livingston when he describes in *The Curse of Tramp Life* (1912, p. 22), his complete disregard for his own mortality in the thrill of hurtling at top speed through the night, hanging underneath a train, death only inches from his face, as the tracks hurtle past beneath him:

> I at last felt that I had given up everything but life itself to please that bane of my existence. ... There, hanging on with only those weak, human hands, out of reach of any possible succour, speeding through the night, I felt at peace with all the world.

The above passage demonstrates the link between the energy of tramping and the energy of writing, but below, Virginia Woolf (1980, p. 132) demonstrates the tensions between the physical momentum of tramping and the act of writing. A note from Woolf's diary captures this standoff between the need to write and the need to be in motion:

> Nothing to record; only an intolerable fit of the fidgets to write away. Here I am chained to my rock: forced to do nothing: doomed to let every wrong, spite, irritation & obsession scratch & claw & come again. This is to say that I may not walk and I must not work.

In the chapter on Woolf in her book *Wanderers: A History of Women Walking*, Kerry Andrews writes at length on this tension between Woolf's need to write and her compulsion to tramp. But before discussing this aspect of the writer, first, a note on Woolf's credentials as a literary vagabond. In spite of being born into a wealthy, upper-class family, Woolf rejected this lifestyle: "Describing herself as a 'tramp,' Woolf associates herself with vagrancy, of existing outside the ordinary bounds of settled society" (Andrews, 2020, pp. 150-160). And in a letter written by Woolf to Violet Dickinson (1975, p. 221), as well as describing a passion for the natural world, there is some evidence that she even may have identified with the ancient Cynics:

> There is a Greek austerity about my life which is beautiful and might go straight into a bas relief. You can imagine that I never wash, or do my hair; but stride with gigantic strides over the wild moorside, shouting odes of Pindar, as I leap from crag to crag, and exulting in the air that buffets me, and caresses me, like a stern but affectionate parent.

Andrews describes the "magic of these states, blended with the powerful 'joy of walking' " as the raw material for Woolf's writing, "the 'fine thin sheet' on which her translucent, cloud-like ideas are both imaginatively and literally impressed." Below, Andrews (2020, pp. 161-162) also acknowledges the tension between walking and writing about Woolf's mental health, which ultimately resulted in her suicide.

> Writing without walking was, for Woolf, inert, dead, 'inanimate'. Only by placing her body into physical animation did she feel capable of animating her words, of giving life to sentences. [...] Being on foot both soothed and stimulated Woolf, keeping quiet the gnawing doubts about her own literary abilities that crept in when her mental health weakened and she became vulnerable to the paralysing depression that struck

from time to time. If she was lucky, her boot-clad feet could outpace her distress.

I make no apologies here for including one further passage from Andrews' thesis on Woolf (2020, pp. 165-169), not only to expand on this important aspect of the vagabond writer's wanderlust but out of respect for Andrew's own writing voice, insightful as it is because of her own compulsion for walking.

> Woolf appears as Prometheus, helpless and 'chained', a victim of the gods' punishment and forced into inactivity while a vulture pecks away at her mind. She is compelled to remain still, inert, unanimated: it is not just phrases and sentences that are left lifeless in the absence of walking. … Walking thereby becomes an important safety mechanism, so that the body, and not the mind, is left 'dusty & hot'. As a result, it is also the means of turning physical energy into intellectual perspicuity: as the body moves, the eye sees, and the words are formed in a seamless, pauseless process. […] So enmeshed were writing and walking for Woolf that she came to see working on a novel as a form of walking. […] walking became the fuel that sustained and fired all her mental activities.

But I leave the final word on the indispensability of walking for the vagabond writer to the Swiss writer and walker Robert Walser. Walser spent the last 27 years of his life in mental institutions after confessing to hallucinating and hearing voices—first continuing with his writing, but after being moved to a different sanatorium against his wishes, he stopped writing and simply walked. On imploring the local inspector of taxes to set his rates at the lowest level possible, the inspector asked why he was always out walking when he should be writing:

> 'Walk,' was my answer, "I definitely must, to invigorate myself and to maintain contact with the living world, without perceiving which I could not write the half of one more single word, or produce the tiniest poem in verse or prose. Without walking, I would be dead, and my profession, which I love passionately, would be destroyed. (Walser, 1992 p. 87)

WHAT THE VAGABOND SEEKS TO ESCAPE FROM

Upon my soul I think that the greatest way of walking, now I consider the matter, or now that I have stumbled upon it, is walking away.

Hilaire Belloc (1911, p. 16)

The attraction to tramp is often matched in equal part by a need to escape the suffocating glue of mainstream society's rules and conventions. Sometimes, the tramp had more pressing reasons to get out on the road, as acknowledged by tramp writer Jim Phelan. When Phelan found himself in danger or difficulty, he noted that it is the tramp's natural impulse to "turn around and head for the horizon." It must be acknowledged then that there are sticks that drive the vagabond to wander, as well as the obvious carrots described above.

The joy in tramping and affinity with nature of another woman tramp writer, Dolly Kennedy Yancey,[1] will be returned to in the next chapter, but below, in the following passage from her book *The Tramp Woman* (1909, pp. 2-3), she describes that other side of wanderlust, precisely what it is that she seeks to escape *from* when she takes to the road:

> Does it pay only to live to accumulate property and junk, which to a traveller would prove expensive 'excess baggage?' Does it pay to harden one's heart against the cultivation of healthy, human instincts, and to live a narrow, selfish life in a conservative community where one is always subjected to unkind criticism? Why unkind? Oh, Conservatism, what sins are committed in thy name!

In the passage below, Thoreau (cited in Belloc, 1911, p. 56) echoes Yancey's sentiments about the need to escape the boredom and oppressive nature of mainstream society:

> I confess that I am astonished at the power of endurance, to say nothing of the moral insensibility, of my neighbours who confine themselves to shops and offices the whole day for weeks and months, ay, and years almost together.

In spite of the strong natural forces that compel people to cultivate and protect their community, the vagabond, like the Cynic, has an equally strong and opposing compulsion to reject its values in what Nietzsche describes as an

---

[1] Yancey's achievements as a tramp and early proponent of feminism are negatively matched by some unashamedly racist comments about African Americans that will shock her modern reader, and certainly outraged this reader. Comments that conflict markedly with the attitudes of most of the other contributors to this book who, from the ancient Cynics onwards, embraced cosmopolitan values unreservedly. But given throughout my research that I only encountered two women tramp writers (although significantly more celebrity women vagabonds), and this is a book about vagabondage, I considered it important not to omit those aspects of Yancey's writing that contribute to the discussion in hand.

unceasing desire for novelty. Here, Nietzsche (1909, p. 25) expresses the same citizen of the world sentiments as Diogenes:

> Why cling to your bit of earth, or your little business, or listen to what your neighbour says? It is so provincial to bind oneself to views which are no longer binding a couple of hundred miles away.

As with Stevenson's essay on walking tours cited above, Thoreau's essay 'Walking' regrets that the average walker is not nearly adventurous enough, noting the phenomena of the tourist hiker as long ago as 1862, and offering advice on ridding ourselves of possessions and commitments in order to become a truly serious walker:

> We are but faint-hearted crusaders; even the walkers nowadays undertake no persevering world's end enterprises. Our expeditions are but tours, and come round again at evening to the old hearthside from which we set out. Half of the walk is but retracing our steps. We should go forth on the shortest walks, perchance, in the spirit of stirring adventure, never to return, prepared to send back our embalmed hearts only as relics to our desolate kingdom. If you have paid your debts and made your will and settled all your affairs, and are a free man, then you are ready for a walk. (Thoreau cited in Rickett, 1906, p. 94)

IS THE VAGABOND BORN OR MADE?

There is one final aspect of wanderlust, indeed the vagabond temperament in general, which those cited in this chapter repeatedly allude to, not least Rickett (1906, p. 3) in the following passage:

> "There are some men born with a vagrant strain in the blood, an inquisitiveness about the world beyond their doors. Natural revolutionaries they, with an ingrained distaste for the routine of ordinary life and the conventions of civilization.

Is adopting the lifestyle of the vagabond, as discussed in this book, a conscious choice or an impulse that cannot be avoided? From the evidence, I allowed for the possibility that the tramp is simply born a tramp through some endogenous but unexplainable sense of "not belonging" or belonging to the world in a different way to his or her fellows. A natural impulse that is not satisfied with the rules and conventions of the society in which they live—a 'condition' also linked to the tramp's natural affinity to nature and to non-human animals, as discussed further in the next chapter. Thoreau (cited in Belloc, 1911, p. 54) has no doubt about the question:

No wealth can buy the requisite leisure, freedom, and independence, which are the capital in this profession. It comes only by the grace of God. It requires a direct dispensation from Heaven to become a walker. You must be born into the family of the Walkers. Ambulator nascitur, non fit [A walker is born, not made].

Sir Walter Scott (cited in Belloc, 1911, pp. 13-14) adds to the evidence that one is born with the natural instinct of wanderlust in his essay 'A Strolling Pedlar.' He describes the early delight he got from all forms of travel, "by far my most favourite amusement," and the alarm and anxiety that his excursions produced in his parents:

> My father used to protest to me on such occasions that he thought I was born to be a strolling pedlar; and though the prediction was intended to mortify my conceit, I am not sure that I altogether disliked it.

I end this chapter with another passage from contemporary vagabond writer Jim Christy's unpublished work, *Wandering Heart*. Christy's description of wanderlust is all the more poignant as it was written from the confines of a hospital wheelchair where Christy, recovering from a stroke, was incapable of responding to those powerful forces calling him to hit the road:

> What I felt sitting in my wheelchair down at the end of that hospital hallway was the lust to wander, pure and simple. I've always wanted to carry my passport with me wherever I go whether to the supermarket or the next town on an errand. I fancy ducking out on my errand, giving up my serious pursuits to head for the airport and buy a ticket anywhere. With my horizons narrowed, I fancy walking out the door and just going with no preconceived notion, no plan, turn left or right it doesn't matter.

> There is sometimes while traveling a powerful feeling of happiness without thinking of happiness, of expanded consciousness and being a part of everything around you. ... My most intense memory of this state of being, perhaps it was what Colin Wilson called the St. Neot's Margin—a feeling of expanded consciousness that came over him while passing through that English town on a bus. For me it was the old bus station in Barcelona some time in the early Seventies while I stood in the big hall waiting to leave for Morocco. I had never been happier or more at ease.

> The feeling can come over you in the most unlikely of places; it is not necessary to be in Tibet or Barcelona. One time, I was sitting on the wooden steps of a general store in Effingham, Illinois, just come down from Chicago, waiting for the bus to St. Louis and bam, all of a sudden I

felt as if I was hovering over the steps, floating above the rooftops, surveying the scene of shops and houses and cars; the small town bicycle world of kids.

It is a credit to Christy that he continued to explore the world and marvel at its wonders long after most Westerners, smug in the knowledge that the world had been mined of its secrets, sat back to glory at their cleverness in university campuses or simply be passive spectators on their ubiquitous TVs and other electronic devices. It is also a sadness to witness the urgency and power with which the vagabonds above have described wanderlust over the past 150 or so years, given the knowledge that such adventures appear to be a less common feature in Western society today.

Chapter 2
AFFINITY WITH NATURE

> Moralists are plentiful, scholars abound, but men in close, vital sympathy with the Earth, a sympathy that comprehends because it loves, and loves because it comprehends, are rare. Let us make the most of them.
>
> Arthur Rickett (1906, p. 113)

> Man must go back to the earth if his race is not to become extinct in the world. He must leave the horrible, crowded noisome cities and go back to the earth. If not he will shrivel up and die out.
>
> Bart Kennedy (1902, p. 111)

Their affinity with the natural world is one of the most recorded aspects of the vagabond temperament from ancient times up to the present. But it is important here to distinguish between the vagabond's relationship to nature with that of, say, the romantic poets. Rickett contrasts the poetic appreciation of the beauties of nature—even though such were also present in many vagabond writers—with "an intellectual enthusiasm for the wonders of the natural world." The vagabond's passion for the earth, he says, differs from the "nature-worship" of poets like Wordsworth and Shelly: "It is less romantic, more realistic ... not so much that of the devotee as that of the lover. There is nothing mystical or abstract about it. It is direct, personal, intimate" (Rickett, 1906, pp. 4-5). This relationship, Rickett continues, is most acutely demonstrated by a deep and tender sympathy for creation more characteristic of the Eastern than the Western mind. And in his chapter on Thoreau, that writer's link to Buddhism is more precisely formulated:

> He [Thoreau] was in sympathy with Eastern modes of regarding life; and the pantheistic tendency of his religious thought, especially his care and reverence for all forms of life, suggest the devout Buddhist. [...] The tenderness of the Buddhist towards the lower creation is not due to sentimentalism, nor is it necessarily a sign of sensitiveness of feeling. (Rickett, 1906, p. 104)

Such links to the vagabond's affinity with nature and links to Buddhism can be traced back to the ancient Cynics, as is evident from their philosophic stance that the key to happiness—or more accurately, a reduction in suffering—can be achieved by mastering our desires: if one desires nothing, one lacks nothing. Trade links existed between the Mediterranean and India during the 100 or so years before Cynicism formally emerged, and Diogenes was reportedly born in 404 BCE, 79 years after the Buddha died in 483 BCE. This philosophic stance becomes most pronounced when discussing the vagabond's relationship to non-human animals.

WHAT CAN HUMANS LEARN FROM ANIMALS

Why should the elemental forces of Nature appeal so strongly to us? Why does the dweller in the open air feel that an unseen bond of sympathy binds him to the lowest forms of sentient life? Why is a St. Francis tender towards animals? Why does a Thoreau take a joy in the company of the birds, the squirrels, and feel a sense of companionship in the very flowers? Nay, more: what is it that gives a Jefferies this sense of communion?

Arthur Rickett (1906, p. 106)

To answer these questions, it would be helpful to look at some of the wider philosophical arguments on the subject. The Cynics, Stoics and Epicureans all held to the belief that true human good lay in the healthy desires experienced by animals (and also that of children before being corrupted by 'education'). The Cynics, in particular, turned to the habits of animals as a source of rhetoric for the most natural way to live. Diogenes' lifestyle, it is said (Laërtius, 1995, p. 25), was inspired by watching a mouse running about: not looking for a place to lie down in, not afraid of the dark, not seeking any of the things which we consider to be dainties. His choice of a large earthenware wine vat as a mobile home was likely inspired by his observation of a snail, a simple lifestyle deliberately adopted to contrast with Western society's obsession with luxury.

Colombian/American philosopher Luis E. Navia proposes that Diogenes' praise of animal nature and his self-characterisation as a dog can be interpreted as an ironic strategy, a kind of inverted and rhetorical allegory to expose, "the absurdity of human conduct when it resembles the behaviour of non-rational beings." Navia's interpretation of the Cynics' use of animals in their teaching is not that animal life is preferable, nor that we should adopt animal life as a model for our own. Rather, we should follow, not deny, our own nature in the same way that animals follow theirs. Instead of following our nature, the Cynic Antisthenes claimed, most humans follow conventions. And it is only by divesting ourselves of the artificiality and superficiality with which we deny our true nature, that a happy and virtuous life can be attained: "We must deface the currency that has made us what we were not meant to be" (Navia, 2001, p. 100).

Thoreau clearly shared the Cynics' use of animal behavior as a more helpful way of approaching human behavior than the pretensions of humans: "Thoreau ... was drawn towards them [animals] because he felt an affinity with them—an affinity more compelling in its attraction than the affinity of the average human person" (Rickett, 1906, p. 107). But Rickett was also keen to point out in what way Thoreau had been popularly misrepresented:

> I am concerned to defend him from the criticism that he was a loveless, brooding kind of creature, more interested in birds and fishes than in his fellow-men. For he was neither loveless nor brooding, and the characteristics that have proved most puzzling arose from the mingled strain in his nature of the Eastern quietist and the shrewd Western. (Rickett, 1906, pp. 92-93)

In complete accord with Navia's analysis above, Rickett emphasizes that Thoreau was drawn towards animals, not because he detected any semblance of humankind in them but because they knew how to live in accordance with nature. This theme is revisited in Rickett's chapter on Richard Jefferies, where that writer declares, "There is nothing human in any living Animal. All Nature, the Universe as far as we see, is anti- or ultra-human outside and has no concern with man." But here Rickett (1906, p. 160) challenges Jefferies:

> why, if the Earth has no concern with man, should it soothe with its benison, and fire his being with such ecstatic rapture? ... [Jefferies] sense of happiness, his delight in the Earth, may no doubt afford him consolation, but it is an irrational comfort, an agreeable delusion.

Whatever his issue with Jefferies, here Rickett has departed from his earlier analysis of Thoreau's rhetoric on the subject and chosen to ignore the distinction between the therapeutic effects that nature has on human beings in general, and arguments used by vagabond writers in his book that most humans have forgotten how to live a natural life in accordance with nature. I do not see that Jefferies has departed from this central argument. But I will end this digression on animals with a quote from the Cynic writer and historian Dio Chrysostom (cited in Dobbin, 2012, p. xxxix) who proposed the same argument 2000 years ago:

> Consider the beasts yonder and the birds, how much freer from trouble they live than men, and how much more happily also, how much healthier and stronger they are, and how much each of them lives the

longest life possible, although they have neither hands nor human intelligence. And yet, to counter-balance these and their other limitations, they have one very great blessing—they own no property.

THE VAGABOND'S PASSION FOR THE NATURAL WORLD

> Every turn of the road gains in interest; every object that meets the eye seems to have some initiative meaning; and when the object itself at last appears, nothing can surpass the delight of flinging one's self on the ground to rest upon the first impression, and to interpose a delicious pause before the final attainment.
>
> Harriet Martineau (1838, p. 55)

As acknowledged by Harriet Martineau, when it comes to the praise of nature, this is something the vagabond shares not only with the Romantic poets but also with hikers and others drawn to the countryside for its therapeutic effects. I will, therefore, keep this section brief as the reader will be no stranger to the writers' admiration of the natural world, their praise of it has been extensively recorded. In the case of the vagabond, however, as with the compulsion to always be in motion, for the most part, being close to nature was as indispensable as the air they breathed. That the natural world fuelled the vagabond's very existence is evident from Martineau's exuberant praise of nature in the quote above. Her flinging herself to the ground from the sheer exhilaration of her encounter with the outdoors is echoed in the following passage by tramp writer Dolly Kennedy Yancey in *The Tramp Woman* (1909, pp. 48-49):

> I would revel in life under a tent the whole summer through. I am a lover of nature, and even were I financially able to procure them, I would eschew some of the habiliments and gewgaws that are so desirable in polite society. ... When I go back West I am going to throw myself down in a field, roll like a dog, and breath pure air. I crave freedom—freedom to grow, to think, to feel, to get out of life all that my God intended.

But rather than overindulge in accolades to the natural landscape, I simply leave the reader with the following two passages from Stephen Graham's *A Tramp's Sketches* (1913, pp. 243-249 and pp. 8-9), leaving as he does powerful testimony to the tramp's restorative relationship to nature:

> I have learned to do without the town, without the great machine that provides man with a living. I have sucked in a thousand rains, and absorbed a thousand suns, lain on many thousand banks of the earth. I

have walked at the foot of mountains along long green valleys, I have climbed great ranges and peeped over them, I have lived in barren and in fertile places, and my road-companion has been Nature herself.

He who sleeps under the stars is bathed in the elemental forces which in houses only creep to us through keyholes. I may say from experience that he who has slept out of doors every day for a month, nay even for a week, is at the end of that time a new man. He has entered into new relationship with the world in which he lives, and has allowed the gentle creative hands of Nature to re-shape his soul.

Less often written about, and so important to acknowledge here, is that in spite of their obvious desire to be close to nature, the reality for many tramp writers were the dangers and harsh conditions that nature dealt out in equal measure to its beneficence.

THE UNSENTIMENTAL SIDE OF NATURE

Although drawn to the natural world for all the reasons outlined above, the tramp writers discussed in *The Golden Age of Tramping*, were at times less effusive about nature than the celebrity writers referred to in Rickett or Andrews's books, and whom, in turn, Rickett described as less sentimental about nature than the romantic poets. This is likely because Rickett's literary vagabonds had an element of choice, sometimes supported by financial security, about when to expose themselves to the harsher elements of nature than the tramp writers did. Morley Roberts, while addicted to nature, does not hold back from describing not only its boring aspects but also its desolation. In his book, *A Tramp's Note-Book,* he criticizes those who sentimentalize nature and targets in particular the vainglory of adventurers who exalt the virtues of 'conquering' nature; elevating themselves vertically from the rest of the human herd, rather than exiling themselves horizontally (and anonymously) as does the tramp:

> very little above the snow-line is truly beautiful. It is often desolate, sometimes intolerably grand and savage, but lovely it is very rarely. It is perhaps against human nature to be there at all. (Roberts, 1904, p. 217)

Bart Kennedy is another tramp writer who shares negative observations concerning the so-called beauty of nature: "to tell the truth, at that time the scenery impressed me but little. It was great and wild and finely coloured. But I had had enough mountain scenery to last me a lifetime." Working hard in the middle of it for two months had probably knocked the poetry out of it. "Neither will fine scenery impress a man when he's hungry, alone, tired, and wondering if he'll get out of it alive." And Kennedy nearly did not come out of it alive. He gives an account of how, alone in the Rockies, he took stock of his life and decided to end it, unslinging his revolver and "determined to take a rest for good and all." Having witnessed how men shot through the brain jump violently, then sink down with a look of peace on their faces, he mapped out the scenario in his mind then placed the muzzle of his revolver under his right ear, "so as to get the base of the brain."

> But just as I put my finger on the trigger I began to think in a way I had never thought before. My whole life, and everything I had done in it, suddenly came up before my mind. Everything was so clear and vivid. I seemed to see things from many sides at once. This is the way that men think when they are drowning, I thought. And I brought down the muzzle of the revolver. But I intended to kill myself nevertheless. However, I'd try and analyse my feelings first. And I sat down on a log and wondered. (Kennedy, 1900, p. 162)

Instead of pulling the trigger, Kennedy stood up and "cursed the earth and everything in it," thinking to himself that one day, "the time would come when men of my breed—men from the gutter—would get even with it." Once more, he put the muzzle of the revolver against his head, but at that moment, something came over him, a feeling he was unable to name. "It wasn't fear; it wasn't remorse. I just wanted to live just wanted to live for no particular reason." (Kennedy, 1900, pp. 162-164)

In the following passage from Jean Genet's *A Thief's Journal* (1964, pp. 63 and 66), at that point in his life at least, we are presented with a characterization of the wandering vagabond giving themselves over to the combined effects of nature and wanderlust in a completely unplanned orgy of both misery and pleasure combined. Here is also an acknowledgement of how the harshness of nature strengthened rather than weakened Genet's vagabond spirit:

> Andalusia was lovely, hot and barren. I went all across it. At that age, fatigue was unknown to me. I carried with me such a burden of sorrow that I was sure my whole life would be spent in wandering. Vagrancy was no longer a detail which would embellish my life, but a reality. I no longer know what I thought, but I know that I offered all my woes to God. In my solitude, remote from men, I came quite close to being all love, all devotion. […] Inland, I went through landscapes of sharp rocks that gnawed at the sky and ripped the azure. This rigid, dry, malicious indigence flouted my own and my human tenderness. Yet it incited me to hardness. I was less alone upon discovering in nature one of my

essential qualities: pride. I wanted to be a rock among rocks. I was happy to be one, and proud.

THE NATURAL WORLD -v- THE CIVILIZED WORLD

> An old oak that has been growing where he stands since before the Reformation, taller than many spires, more stately than the greater part of mountains, and yet a living thing, liable to sicknesses and death, like you and me: is not that in itself a speaking lesson in history? But acres on acres full of such patriarchs contiguously rooted, their green tops billowing in the wind, their stalwart younglings pushing up about their knees: a whole forest, healthy and beautiful, giving colour to the light, giving perfume to the air: what is this but the most imposing piece in nature's repertory?
>
> R. L. Stevenson (1904, p. 64)

Leaving aside all of civilizations' other claims, Stevenson reminds us that for all human's architectural achievements alone they can never surpass the achievements of the living non-human world. The previous chapter discussed the effects that mainstream society has as a trigger for wanderlust, something the vagabond is compelled to escape *from* as opposed to the compulsive draw of wanderlust for pleasure and adventure. Here, I will discuss these same dual forces as they apply specifically to the dichotomy between the natural and the man-made world. Graham (1913, p. 41) refers to tramps as "rebels against modern life" and "the first searchers for new life" and notes that we could all benefit from a little more simplicity and "living in communion with Nature." A theme he repeats in *The Gentle Art of Tramping* (1926, p. 86):

> You will discern that going tramping is at first an act of rebellion; only afterwards do you get free from rebelliousness as Nature sweetens your mind. Town makes men contentious; the country smoothes out their souls.

The identical sentiments were expressed by Sydney Smith in his essay 'Walking an Antidote to City Poison' (cited in Belloc, 1911, p. 18):

> As the body, harassed with the noxious air of cities, seeks relief in the freedom and the purity of the fields and hills, so the mind, wearied by commerce with men, resumes its vigour in solitude, and repairs its dignity.

Thoreau (cited in Belloc, 1911, p. 76) takes an even more extreme attitude to the harmful effects of civilization, for him, the wilder and more hostile the territory he inhabits, the better he feels he is able to find the relief he craves from civilization:

> Life consists with wildness. The most alive is the wildest. Not yet subdued to man, its presence refreshes him. One who pressed forward incessantly and never rested from his labours, who grew fast and made infinite demands on life, would always find himself in a new country or wilderness, and surrounded by the raw material of life. ... Hope and the future for me are not in lawns and cultivated fields, not in towns and cities, but in the impervious and quaking swamps.

But not all vagabonds need the respite of the unspoiled wilderness to soothe their troubled soul; William Hazlitt (cited in Belloc, 1911, pp. 27-28) finds respite from the torment of civilization in the anonymity of a country inn:

> Oh, it is great to shake off the trammels of the world and of public opinion; to lose our importunate, tormenting, everlasting personal identity in the elements of nature, and become the creature of the moment, clear of all ties; to hold to the universe only by a dish of sweetbreads, and to owe nothing but the score of the evening; and no longer seeking for applause and meeting with contempt, to be known by no other title than the gentleman in the parlour! [...] An inn restores us to the level of nature, and quits scores with society!

HOW TO *BE* IN NATURE

Staying with Hazlitt, for those considering sampling the vagabond life, it is worth concluding this chapter with some simple advice from two of our literary vagabonds on the best way to fully appreciate taking a break from civilization. On Hazlitt's line, "When I'm in the country, I wish to vegetate like the country," Robert Louis Stevenson (cited in Belloc, 1911, p. 161) concludes the following:

> which is the gist of all that can be said upon the matter. There should be no cackle of voices at your elbow, to jar on the meditative silence of the morning. And so long as a man is reasoning he cannot surrender himself to that fine intoxication that comes of much motion in the open air, that begins in a sort of dazzle and sluggishness of the brain, and ends in a peace that passes comprehension.

And John Burroughs (cited in Belloc, 1911, pp. 231-232) offers some encouragement on just what the vagabond traveler might hope to experience if they are able to give themselves over totally to the tramping lifestyle:

> His pores are all open, his circulation is active, his digestion good. His heart is not cold, nor his faculties asleep. He is the only real traveller; he alone tastes the 'gay, fresh sentiment of the road.' ... The vital, universal currents play through him. He knows the ground is alive; he feels the pulses of the wind, and reads the mute language of things. His sympathies are all aroused; his senses are continually reporting messages to his mind. Wind, frost, rain, heat, cold, are something to him. He is not merely a spectator of the panorama of nature, but a participator in it. He experiences the country he passes through—tastes it, feels it, absorbs it ...

ASCETICISM AND THE ABJECT

> Look at me, I have no home, no city, no property, no slave; I sleep on the ground; I haven't a wife or children; no officer's quarters, only earth, sky — and one tattered cloak. What more do I need? I am cheerful, I am tranquil, and I am free. You never see me fail to get what I want, or get stuck with what I want to avoid.
>
> <div align="right">Epictetus, <i>Discourse on Cynicism</i>
(c. 50 – 135 CE, cited in Dobbin, 2012, p. 167)</div>

Rickett's chapter on William Hazlitt touches on the vagabond's relationship to the abject as it links to their affinity with nature and the animal world. Using the analogy that fine plants are produced from soil treated with dung, he makes the argument that genius should not be dismissed because it comes from the hands and mind of the vagabond:

> The soil of the rose garden may be manured with refuse that Nature uses in bringing forth the lovely bloom of the rose. ... And so from unhealthy stock, from temperaments affected by disease, have sprung the roses of genius—transformed by the mysterious alchemy of the imagination into pure and lovely things. There are, of course, poisonous flowers, just as there is a type of genius—not the highest type—that is morbid. But this does not affect my contention that genius is not necessarily morbid because it may have sprung from a morbid soil. (Hazlitt, cited in Rickett, 1906, pp. 22-23)

As I noted in my work on Cynicism, "this living on the edge of society and courting indecency, defilement and death—is as much about embracing a positive identity, as it is about simply cocking a snoot at convention." It is helpful here to consider Julia Kristeva's work, *Powers of Horror: an essay on abjection* (1982), where she maintains that we are defined by the things that disgust us; the waste of our own bodies is expelled in order that we may live. Our world exists on one side of the border between our living being and the ultimate waste of our own corpses.

Samuel Beckett's unnamed creature in his novella *The End*, provides a powerful example of the vagabonds' existence in this abject borderland, maintaining the minimum necessary to sustain life. His hero ultimately gives up the comfort of a pigsty to a pig to find warmth and shelter in a dung heap (Beckett, 1980, pp. 79-80). In Diogenes' case—as much a philosophical declaration as a personal lifestyle choice—in his indifference to the waste of his own body, he marks himself out from the pretensions of human beings' sham sophistication. He reinforces his own position on the margins of society, a society which in turn rejects his Cynic lifestyle as base and inhuman in order to reinforce its own 'higher' level of functioning. When Diogenes pisses, farts, defecates and masturbates in public, he is simply holding up a mirror to the the artificial conventions of society around him. As Peter Sloterdijk (1988, p. 151) comments:

> Diogenes is the only Western philosopher who we know consciously and publicly performed his animal business, and there are reasons to interpret this as a component of a pantomimic theory. It hints at a consciousness of nature that assigns positive values to the animal side of human beings and does not allow any dissociation of what is low or embarrassing. Those who do not want to admit that they produce refuse ... risk suffocating one day in their own shit.

A theme also acknowledged by French philosopher Jacques Lacan (2001, p.189):

> The characteristic of a human being is that—and this is very much in contrast with other animals—he doesn't know what to do with his shit. . . . Occupying an uncertain and troubling space between a nature that is never surpassed and a culture that is never closed off, shit defines civilisation.

It follows, then, that by embracing the abject (Diogenes pissing, passing wind, and defecating in public; Hipparchia, the Cynic wife of Crates licking clean the purulent sores of the sick), certain Cynics would have attained spiritual and moral freedom unavailable to those of us who define our humanness by our need to exclude the abject from our thoughts or actions. It also removed any possibility of an Icarian collapse, as the Cynics' asceticism left them with nowhere to fall. Of course, Diogenes well understood that humans had higher mental functions than lower animals, but this made their metaphysical pretensions all the more irrational. The Cynics were not abject but beyond abjection, and the link between their public behavior and personal philosophy can be interpreted as a form of high rhetoric. Other philosophers use formal lectures and theoretical models to share their philosophies, but as the Cynic regards such dialogue as hot air, they simply pass wind by way of a critique. In her work *How to Observe Morals and Manners*, Harriet Martineau (1838, p. 57) makes a plea for the wealthy philosopher to try out the aesthetic lifestyle as a way of connecting with the pleasures that she believes can only be experienced by traveling in vagabond fashion:

> If the wealthy scholar and philosopher could make himself a citizen of the world for the time, and go forth on foot, careless of luxury, patient of fatigue, and fearless of solitude, he would be not only of the highest order of tourists, but a benefactor to the highest kind of science; and he would become familiarized with what few are acquainted with,—the best pleasures, transient and permanent, of travel.

I will conclude this section with a passage from George Orwell's *Down and Out in Paris and London* (2021, p. 16), in which he assists in explaining this link between poverty and peace of mind:

> the great redeeming feature of poverty ... [is] that it annihilates the future ... the less money you have, the less you worry. When you have a hundred francs in the world you are liable to the most craven panics. When you have only three francs you are quite different; for three francs will feed you till tomorrow, and you can't think further than that. [...] And there is another feeling that is a great consolation in poverty. I believe everyone who has been hard up has experienced it. It is a feeling of relief, almost of pleasure, at knowing yourself genuinely down and out. You have talked so often of going to the dogs—[an unintended reference to the Cynics] and well, here are the dogs, and you have reached them, and you can stand it. It takes off a lot of anxiety.

Chapter 3

THE URBAN VAGABOND

> The history of both rural and urban walking is a history of freedom and of the definition of pleasure. But rural walking has found a moral imperative in the love of nature that has allowed it to defend and open up the countryside. Urban walking has always been a shadier business, easily turning into soliciting, cruising, promenading, shopping, rioting, protesting, skulking, loitering, and other activities.
>
> Rebecca Solnit (2001, pp. 173-174)

In spite of the vagabond writers' praise of nature and their warnings about the harmful effects of city life, as with the ancient Cynic, and for that matter, the American hobo, the vagabond is continually drawn back to urban surroundings. Solnit's remark about "the moral imperative of the love of nature" should in no way diminish the powerful writing stimulated by urban landscapes, their inhabitants and visitors. And it is the unique perspective of city life, as penned by the urban vagabond writer, that is the focus of this chapter.

It is a common theme of tramp literature that the wandering vagabond admits to getting bored with nature at times, but then they seem to get bored by just about any condition that cannot sustain their desire for the extraordinary—and city life certainly has its share of the exotic. As tramp writer Stephen Graham (1913, p. 40) acknowledges:

> It is true the wanderer often feels bored, even in beautiful places. I am bored some days every year, no matter where I spend them, and I shall always be. I get tired of this world and want another. That is a common feeling, if not often analysed.

Truly cosmopolitan communities, so important to both the Cynic and modern vagabond (in terms of the merging of different cultures and racial groups within a single, confined geographical area), only truly existed, and still do to a large extent, in larger cities and port towns, thus providing an environment in which the vagabond, and all those presenting as 'different,' were less conspicuous and invited less negative attention than they did in rural towns and villages. In this sense, the city often functioned as a place of refuge, which was particularly the case for the American hobo of the late 1800s. At the height of the depression eras, large numbers of tramps, and also homeless transient workers with money to burn from harvesting, logging, mining, and construction work created urban centers of their own within America's larger cities, with Chicago as its cultural and entertainment capital. At its peak, it was estimated that there were 75,000 transients in Chicago's "Main Stem" alone, an area centered for half a mile in every direction around West Madison Street:

> This city within a city included cheap saloons, restaurants, flophouses, whorehouses, gambling dens, clothing, cigar and drug stores, but also bookstores, theatres, missions and meeting halls, thus providing evidence that the tramp army included those from cultured as well as the laboring classes. (Cutler, 2020, p. ix)

Paradoxically, in the same way, that hobos flocked to these tramp cities for temporary relief and distraction, so too did they become a regular destination for those seeking thrills and escape from their sanitized, mainstream lives in suburbia.

BOHEMIANISM

The 'bohemian' in its modern sense (not to be confused with natives of the Czech region of Bohemia) is popularly considered a very distinct character from the tramp, yet as the title of Thomas Manning Page's book, *Bohemian Life; or The Autobiography of a Tramp* (1884), suggests, the tramp can adopt a dual lifestyle. After an early life on the road tramping in the wilderness and hanging out in tramp jungles, Page spent several years as a struggling artist in Paris before returning to New York, where he founded a "Bohemian Club" in the 1870s, only later to return briefly to tramping. The activities of this motley society, their buffoonery, feasting, and drunken poetry readings, have parallels with the Dadaists who would not appear for a further 40 years. Yet Arthur Rickett (1906, p. 8) makes a disparaging distinction between the two, commenting that the bohemian:

> lacks the rough virility, the sturdy grit, which is the most attractive quality of the best Vagabond. ... At heart the Bohemian is not really unconventional; he is not nomadic by instinct as is the Vagabond.

Noting later (1906, pp. 9-10):

> Far more pronounced in its neurotic character is Modern Bohemianism—as I prefer to call the 'town Vagabond.' The decadent movement in literature has produced many interesting artistic figures,

but they lack the grit and the sanity of outlook which undoubtedly marks the Vagabond.

A clear difference between vagabondage and the popular, modern understanding of bohemianism there certainly was, particularly with respect to the more wealthy or aristocratic bohemian or *haute bohème*. But I disagree with Rickett's descriptions of the bohemian in general as a lesser "superficial character" or a "a town-made imitation" of the vagabond (even if some of the *haute bohème* undoubtedly were). One only has to read Jean-Paul Clébert's *Paris Vagabond* to appreciate the hardships and grit with which some city vagabonds suffered to maintain their lifestyle, further evidence of which is available from George Orwell's *Down and Out in Paris and London*, when that writer adopted the role of the vagabond bohemian—certainly not from necessity—adopting also the Cynic lifestyle of the ascetic as he describes in the passage at the end of the last chapter.

In his comprehensive study of the origins, history, traditions and everyday life of the Gypsy, Jean-Paul Clébert (1964, p. 10) notes that the term 'Bohemian' can be traced back to the Middle Ages in association with both Gypsies and vagabonds in general:

> The name of 'Bohemians' became attached to that of the Goliards, [1] and before long the two terms meant the same. In the fifteenth century, when the first Gypsies put in an appearance on their travels in Central Europe, in colourful array not unlike that of the vagabonds, it was quite natural that this should serve to give them their name. The first written mention of the word 'Bohemian'—undoubtably meaning 'Gypsy'—would seem to be in Pechon de Ruby's [2] book *La Vie Généreux de Mercelots, Gueux, et Boesmiens* [The Generous Life of Pedlars, Beggars and Bohemians (or Gypsies)] (1596).

---

[1] Goliards were wandering medieval students and clerics in the UK, France and Germany, during the 12th and 13th centuries. They were known for their satirical Latin poetry, hedonistic lifestyle, and stand against orthodox Christian ethics.

[2] Pechon de Ruby was a pseudonym which, according to Clébert, was fifteenth-century slang for "wicked child" but translated by Ruby as "Awakened Child". Ruby was the son of an influential father but, at the age of ten, decided to "live his own life" and escaped over the walls of the family's manor house from where he took to the road and embarked on the life of a vagabond. This included learning Gypsy vernacular and being initiated into their syndicated lifestyle. Clébert claims that the book was probably written around 100 years before its first publication in 1596. Clébert, Jean-Paul., *The Gypsies*, London: Readers Union, 1964, pp. 37-38.

But it is not within the scope of this book to open up a discussion on Gypsies, of which there are already numerous excellent volumes available. Even though clear links do exist between Gypsies and vagabondage, theirs is and remains a very specific story and lifestyle that does not fit the central themes of this work. For the purposes of the discussion here, I will confine Bohemianism to refer to its nineteenth and twentieth-century significance and principally to its presentation in urban surroundings.

American writer Henry Miller was another bohemian down and out in Paris around the same time as George Orwell and Blaise Cendrars; the latter a close friend. Miller was later credited as a major influence on Beat Generation writers. Miller went to live in Paris in 1930, only months after Orwell had returned to London. Miller would stay in Paris for 10 years, Orwell stayed in Paris for 18 months. Although the two writers had corresponded, they met only once, and at a time when both were relatively unknown (Miller was writing *Tropic of Cancer* at the time, a book that was censored in both Britain and America until 1961 on the grounds of obscenity). The meeting was in Paris on 23rd December 1936 (three years after Orwell's *Down and Out in Paris and London* had been published) and when Orwell was passing through Paris on his way to fight for the Republicans in the Spanish Civil War. In his book *Henry Miller Down and out in Paris* (1936), Miller's friend George Wickes provides an early account of Miller's own urban vagabond credentials, based on letters written to him by Miller at the time, as well as from *Tropic of Cancer* and other sources. Miller spells out on the first page of *Tropic of Cancer* (2001, p. 1) just how arriving in Paris would change his personal life and writing style: "I have no money, no resources, no hopes. I am the happiest man alive. A year ago, six months ago, I thought I was an artist. I no longer think about it, I just am." And from Millers' first letter to Wickes, written only three days following his arrival in Paris, we have a more precise account of Millers' first impressions of that city, signaling the *flâneur* and writer he would become and in what way, for him, Paris differed from New York and London:

> To know Paris is to know a great deal. How vastly different from New York! What eloquent surprises at every turn of the street. To get lost here is the adventure extraordinary. The streets sing, the stones talk. The houses drip history, glory, romance. ... Here is the greatest congregation of bizarre types. People do dress as they please, wear beards if they like, and shave if they choose. You don't feel that lifeless presence of dull regimentation as in N.Y. and London. (Wickes, 1974, p. 6)

But to return to the older literary vagabonds, later in Rickett's book, he has to acknowledge that, as with the tramp writers in my earlier book, his vagabond writers were as drawn to city streets as they were to the wilderness. Indeed, as with Graham's sentiments above, too much time in either seems to create a compulsion for a change of scenery:

> Although a passion for the Earth is a prevalent note in the character of the literary Vagabond, yet while harking to the call of the country, he is by no means deaf to the call of the town. With the exception of Thoreau, who seemed to have been insensible to any magic save that of the road and woodland, our literary Vagabonds have all felt and confessed to the spell of the city. (Rickett, 1906, p. 37)

And it is in the city that the vagabond writer—tramp and celebrity alike—may embrace bohemianism but, more fascinatingly, has developed an identity and particular writing style that has entertained the reader for a century and a half. Not that other writers have not similarly been connoisseurs of street life going all the way back to the ancient Greeks.

THE *FLÂNEUR*

Charles Baudelaire is among those credited with first identifying the activity of *flânerie*, in turn influenced by Edgar Allan Poe's urban stalker, the practitioner of which, the *flâneur*, has been popularly associated with: a male of the leisured class sauntering around urban environments, a dilettante observer of modern life. The passage below from Baudelaire's 1863 essay, *The Painter of Modern Life* (1964, p. 9), identifies this character as he originally conceived it:

> The crowd is his element, just as the air is that of the birds and water of fishes. His passion and his profession are to become one flesh with the crowd. For the perfect flâneur, for the passionate spectator, it is an immense joy to set up house in the heart of the multitude, amid the ebb and flow of movement, in the midst of the fugitive and the infinite. To be away from home and yet to feel oneself everywhere at home; to see the world, to be at the centre of the world, and yet to remain hidden from the world—such are a few of the slightest pleasures of those independent, passionate, impartial natures which the tongue can but clumsily define. The spectator is a prince who everywhere rejoices in his incognito. ... Thus the lover of universal life enters into the crowd as though it were an immense reservoir of electrical energy. Or we might liken him to a mirror as vast as the crowd itself; or to a kaleidoscope gifted with consciousness, responding to each one of its movements and reproducing the multiplicity of life and flickering grace of all the elements of life.

When Baudelaire describes sensations such as "to feel everywhere at home," "to be at the centre of the world," "the lover of universal life," he could equally be describing the Cynic concept of cosmopolitanism: the rejection of provincial notions of statehood or belonging to a narrowly defined community, to adopt in its place the identity of a 'citizen of the universe.' Writing by those who clearly practiced the art of the *flâneur* can be identified in the late 1800s and early 1900s, yet are neither exclusively male nor from the higher, leisured echelons of society. The writing below from some of the best practitioners of this art (in the following examples on the city of London) serves better to illustrate *flânerie* than any further explanations I could make.

As well as tramping across continents by way of the remotest topography (5,000 miles in the Russian wilderness alone), tramp writer Stephen Graham was a *flâneur par excellence*. In his books *New York Nights* (1927) and *London Nights* (1929), he presents detailed sketches of every aspect of nightlife in those two cities during the 1920s: markets, eating establishments, speakeasies, dosshouses, cemeteries, waterways, tunnels under waterways, red-light districts, theatre-land, and fascinatingly, the high and low life attracted to these places. Graham also employed an entirely novel method of exploring both familiar and unfamiliar city streets, which he describes as 'zig-zag walking.' This involved taking the first turn on the left and the next on the right, continuing in this manner to see where you end up. "In towns this gives you a most alluring adventure. You get into all manner of obscure courts and alleys you would never have noticed in the ordinary way." (1926, p. 53)

Nothing in the city escaped Graham's forensic surveillance, and below are three passages that illustrate both the object of this surveillance and Graham's writing style. The first is from a London cemetery, which he describes as a, "vision of poverty and degradation":

> I watch a man with a bag of fishes' heads trying to coax the stray cats of High Street, Bloomsbury, to come and feed from him. But as most of the cats were sleeping on the tombs of St. Giles' he followed into the churchyard and began to call: 'puss, puss, mew, mew.' Three women were sitting on a bench there, and one had her hair down and was combing it with a broken comb, one was asleep with her chin on her bosom, but the third was watching.
>
> 'Wot is it?' she cried to the man with the bag. 'Don't give it to the cats, give it ver me. I 'aven't 'ad a bite since mornin'. Garn, don't give it to the cats.'
>
> 'Not fit to eat,' said the man with the bag.
>
> 'Is it cat's meat?' asked the woman, 'Give it 'ere.'

But the man went on and called the cats who left the grave of 'unparalleled Pendrell,' succourer of King Charles in the oak tree, left the playground where children romp over what was once the 'plague pit' of St. Giles, and leisurely and suspiciously approached the bag and sniffed at it, not nearly so ready to take what was in it as the outcast woman on the bench. (Graham, 1929, pp. 122-123)

Another side of London nightlife is described in the chapter titled 'Café Bars':

Great Windmill Street is one of the capitals of all-night pleasure, and if one wanders up that narrow Soho lane just after the theatres empty, to the corner where the clock of the Red Lion public house shows the witching hour of night, one is in the midst of foreign Bohemian life.

The back exit of the Lyric Theatre is flanked by the charming 'Stage Door' resort, served by theatrical ladies, and also by the Armenian Café, with its clanking of dominoes and its Easterns sipping thick Turkish coffee ... Opposite is the 'Roma,' a comfortable little bar where chorus girls and supers often resort to discuss their domestic troubles and rivalries over a cup of coffee and a bun. ... Opposite the 'Red Lion' ... is the entrance to a little blind alley called Ham Yard, a place of great activity. At first site you think it is merely the entrance to a garage. But it is something very much more. It is one of the chief centres of night club life. ... when you follow a car in by the narrow way you come into a gaily-lighted open court which is jingling with music and song, while overhead, laughter and the noise of merriment surges upward to the dull sky. (Graham, 1929, pp. 147-148)

Here, Graham digresses into discussing nightclubs. To return to the café bars, we hear about 'Au Chat Noir,' 'Roma,' Caiffa,' 'The Wooden Soldier,' and 'Round the Clock,' as well as places simply referring to street numbers such as " 'Café Bar No. 10' in Denham Street and 'Café No. 21' in Frith Street." And so Graham continues, but without naming each of the "thirty or forty" café bars he says exist at the beginning of the chapter. *London Nights* even includes a chapter titled 'Prison Nights' drawn from several years Graham spent as a nightly prison visitor. The chapter concludes with the following words that emphasize both Graham's arresting prose style and his satirical social commentary:

It is a human Zoo, all the birds and animals of prey are in their cages and many of them have had their claws cut and talons drawn. They are harmless and defeated. There is only one lasting delusion, which is, that we can tame them and make them domestic and useful. They go out at given intervals, but are nearly always sent back. In and out they swarm, the many thousands of the 'known to the police.' (Graham, 1929, p. 121)

The following passage from tramp writer Jim Phelan's *Tramping the Toby* (1955, pp. 61–62), again predominantly an inhabiter of the open road, provides a further example of the tramp-*flâneur's* observation on London street life:

> It is a place of drifters, even if they live in cities. Bookshops crowd one another, and flocks of customers ... bustle in and out. At one end all the shop-windows are filled with music sheets, and all the crooked small alleys are filled with gossiping musicians. ... At the other side the narrow streets and alleys lead into Soho. Chinese and negroes, French people and Greeks and folks of a hundred nationalities move in and out of Soho ... Brass plates, squares of wood, or visiting cards held in place by drawing pins, indicate the offices of a thousand specialists. tattoo artists and private detectives, theatrical agents and dancing schools, Chinese laundries and dealers in "rare" books, all function side by side. There may be ordinary shops and offices, too. But I saw none of them that morning. I only saw the seething, multicoloured, polyglot, exotic crowd, like the populace of some giant paddincan [tramp hostelry], at a crossroads where all the highways of the world converge. It is a wonderful street for a tramp to walk through.

As for the woman *flâneur* (or *flâneuse*), one of the most powerful examples of this genre, with parallels to Graham and Phelan's observations of London, is that provided in Virginia Woolf's 1930 essay 'Street Haunting,' "to escape is the greatest of pleasures; street haunting in winter the greatest of adventures." Fuelled by the energy of walking, the essay has to be read to be appreciated but setting off into London's streets at night—even if it is on the sometimes forgotten pretext of buying a pencil—Woolf is assaulted by all the sights, smells and sounds (including fragments of conversations) the City has to offer, its physical and animal delights and absurdities, in motion or stationary, both sides of lit windows, changing at every street corner, and what cannot be known is subjected to Woolf's vivid and digressionary imagination. Here, Woolf (1930, pp. 2-5) describes shifting from the familiarity of her home into the anonymity of the street and the change this has on her identity:

> As we step out of the house on a fine evening between four and six, we shed the self our friends know us by and become part of that vast republican army of anonymous trampers, whose society is so agreeable after the solitude of one's own room. For there we sit surrounded by objects which perpetually express the oddity of our own temperaments

and enforce the memories of our own experience. [...] But when the door shuts on us, all that vanishes.

Then, out into the streets and Woolf (1930, pp. 6-7) combines witnessing with imagination:

> How beautiful a London street is then, with its islands of light, and its long groves of darkness, and on one side of it perhaps some tree-sprinkled, grass-grown space where night is folding herself to sleep naturally and, as one passes the iron railing, one hears those little cracklings and stirrings of leaf and twig which seem to suppose the silence of fields all round them ... But this is London, we are reminded; high among the bare trees are hung oblong frames of reddish yellow light—windows; there are points of brilliance burning steadily like low stars—lamps; this empty ground, which holds the country in it and its peace, is only a London square, set about by offices and houses where at this hour fierce lights burn over maps, over documents, over desks where clerks sit turning with wetted forefinger the files of endless correspondences; or more suffusedly the firelight wavers and the lamplight falls upon the privacy of some drawing-room, its easy chairs, its papers, its china, its inlaid table, and the figure of a woman, accurately measuring out the precise number of spoons of tea ...

Kerri Andrews discusses *Street Haunting* in her book *Wanderers: A History of Women Walking*. Referring to Woolf's description of "that vast republican army of anonymous trampers" she encounters on hitting the streets of London, the sheer number of whom, Andrews observes, "are sufficient to challenge the existing social order." And here Andrews (2020, pp. 173-174) echos the opening quote of this chapter from Solnit when she comments:

> Woolf picks up on long-held views of walking not only as dangerous but legally suspect—there is little distance between a 'tramp', who might be hauled before a magistrate for vagrancy because he is walking the land, and a 'tramper' —a walker who has the power to disrupt the social order. ... she [Woolf] describes how walking smashes the brittle social structures in which individuals clothe themselves. On leaving the house, and entering the community of 'trampers': 'The shell-like covering which our souls have excreted to house themselves, is broken'

Individual identities, Andrews observes, are broken down so that all that is left is this ability to perceive the outside world through an eye common to all streetwalkers and observers, "able to construct whatever it wants, and to be whatever it wants." In this sense, then we all become *flâneurs*, at the same time, both the watchers and the watched, both wandering and wondering.

Another example of the *flâneuse* discussed by Andrews is Anaïs Nin. In a diary entry of Nin's when that writer was only 16 years old, Nin comments on the way that promenading men and women interacted to attract attention, commenting, "It was all very funny and very dumb at the same time." From this commentary, Andrews (2020, p. 207) draws the following observations: "The entire episode hinges on Nin's subtle observations of the complex interactions between various types of walking and various types of watching. Only language is capable of capturing the mechanics of the relationship between the two". Having reached adulthood in New York, Andrews informs us that it was not until Nin moved to Paris in 1924, now aged 26, that she began to hone her observational writing and that by 1966, her diaries consisted of 150 volumes, taking up two five-drawer filing cabinets in a Brooklyn bank vault. We are further informed that a large part of this writing, from the many locations of Nin's itinerant life, "documented how she moved and felt and lived in urban spaces." Nin would continue writing her diaries for a further 11 years before her death from cancer.

> Her journal documents among other things, the importance of walking to Nin's life, from its function as a mechanism to manage her emotional health, to the role it played in her writing, to its involvement in the ways she expressed and experienced her sexuality. (Andrews, 2020, p. 210)

Four years on from Virginia Woolf's essay *Street Haunting*, a 1934 diary entry Nin made in the same city, London, confirms both of these women writers' entitlement to the designation *flâneuse*, undermining the popular belief that such a condition is an exclusively male preserve: "I find myself walking the streets … fascinated by houses, windows, doorways, by the face of a bootblack, by a whore, by the dreary rain, by a gaudy dinner at the Regents Palace, by Fitzroy's Tavern." (Nin cited in Andrews, 2020, p. 211) Note the similarity here between the objects of Nin's fascination and that of their male counterparts, Graham and Phelan. But to return to Andrews' (and Solnit's) concern about women walking the streets being open to a misinterpretation of their motives:

> Most accounts of walking in the city see urban walking as extremely dangerous for women because of a perceived risk of sexual assault, and the additional possibility that, historically at least, a respectable woman walking the streets might be mistaken for a prostitute—the archetypal 'streetwalker'. (Andrews, 2020, p. 214)

The latter may well have been the case, but a woman walking alone in the wilderness was arguably at greater risk from sexual assault, as the episode described by Andrews in her chapter on Cheryl Strayed illustrates: that writer was accosted at the end of her 1100 mile lone trek along the Pacific Crest Trail. And, as described in Chapter 1, Kathleen Phelan's first solo tramp through 20 countries clearly exposed her to similar dangers. Reluctant as she was to write about the numerous occasions she was molested by men, the few she does recount happened mainly between urban centers, not in them.

Women hobos often disguised themselves as men to avoid unwanted attention, even to obtain casual work only available to men, and young male hobos (prushuns), some not yet in their teens, were the victims of predatory older tramps (jockers) ostensibly to 'protect' them but more likely to assist in petty criminality or to sexually abuse them.[3] Thousands of adult and child hobos lost their lives or were injured, including tramp writer William Henry Davies, who lost a foot jumping a train headed for the Klondike. Many others, including most of the tramp writers, featured in my earlier work, served jail time, assaults and other degradations.

Enough here, then, to simply acknowledge that vagabondage has its seedy and brutal side as well as its pleasures and joys. Kathleen Phelan experienced both, but her writing mainly focuses on the positive side of tramping, and paradoxically, outmoded male chivalry seems to have neutralized some of Phelan's trickier escapades. She also had the advantage of getting by in 13 languages acquired during her global ramblings, including Arabic, Urdu, Spanish, French, Italian and Scandinavian, all of which served her well. For the most part, Phelan's writing is dominated by the sheer pleasure and excitement of being out on the road and, in the spirit of the *flâneur*—the phenomena under discussion here—the following is a sample of her own fascinations with city life; in this case Ataba Square, Cairo:

> One side of the square small streets led past the opera House and widened into boulevards with fashionable cafés and shops, luxury hotels, and beyond that, the Nile. On the other side, the narrow streets disappeared into a network of lanes and alleys which held the noisy, colourful bazaars and markets, thronged with people.
>
> Suddenly there came a thudding of hooves and warning shouts. Lorries braked, a tram bell clanged urgently and men, women and children

---

[3] See Flynt, Josiah. 'Homosexuality Among Tramps,' Appendix A in Havelock Ellis, *Studies in the Psychology of Sex*, Volume 2, Sexual Inversion, Philadelphia: F.A. Davis Company, 1927

scattered swiftly. Swooping into the square came a herd of about 40 camels headed by a small one on which perched a laughing young Arab.

He sat proudly showing off his ability to control and direct the herd between the traffic. The crowd roared their admiration for this man who had ridden straight in from the desert.

As he swept across the square to pass me, I made the age-old sign holding up my right hand palm outwards on a level with my face. It is known as the 'show-out' which means 'Good luck to you.' He then lowered his hand but immediately swept it up and this time, he held his hand still palm outwards but farther away from his face, which meant 'need any help?'

I at once crossed my arms, hiding my hands, which indicated to him that I did not need anything. These greetings were made swiftly and unobtrusively and he nodded gravely and was gone.

That was a great moment. There I stood, a stranger in Cairo, coming from the other side of the world, and yet I was able to change greetings with a wandering Arab camel-driver. He probably had centuries of nomadic history. I had only my lifetime, but we were able to communicate because we both follow the road. (Phelan, K.,1972)

A NOTE ON PSYCHOGEOGRAPHY

The more recent artistic and literary genre identified as psychogeography, is credited to the Letterist and Situationist movements of the 1950s. Psychogeography is closely related to *dérive* walking: unplanned drifting through urban landscapes with no preconceived expectations other than the promise of coming upon some novel experience—as described in Stephen Graham's 'zig-zag walking' above.[4] For all intent and purposes, then, psychogeography owes its derivation to *flânerie* and beyond, only adding to the object of its interest the ongoing industrialization and development of urban landscapes beyond city centers—together with the aesthetic effects that these man-made environments have on those who use and inhabit them. Those who wish to explore this particular development of *flânerie* further should refer to Walter Benjamin's (1892–1940) uncompleted work *The Arcades Project* (written between 1927 and 1940 and published posthumously in 1982). For the origins

---

[4] Unconnected with psychogeography, other methods have been devised for allowing random explorations through urban spaces such as that of the French writer, photographer and conceptual artist Sophie Calle, who followed random strangers even across international boundaries.

of psychogeography itself, see (Letterist) Guy Debord's 'Introduction to a Critique of Urban Geography' published in *Les Lèvres Nues* #6 (September 1955)—both Benjamin's and Debord's texts are freely available as digital downloads.

W. G. Sebald's *Rings of Saturn* (1995) did much to kickstart a renewed interest in walking-inspired ethnographic writing. Beware, though, of the many claims by book reviewers comparing new writers to Sebald, for the most part, these should be given little regard. As with those who talk about Beckettian writers, Sebald was a uniquely unique writer to be enjoyed, not emulated. See the chapter below titled 'Fact or Fiction,' of which Sebald was a master at blending seamlessly. The genre has been taken forward in recent times by writers such as Iain Sinclair, Will Self and Lucy (formally Luc) Sante—the recent transgendering of the latter provides some relief from this seemingly bloke-dominated fraternity of ambulatory writers.

But this is a book about vagabond writers, most of whom did not identify with any particular genre and, although exemplifying the characteristics of psychogeography at its best, did so way before the term ever came into popular usage. The vagabond writers discussed elsewhere in this book wrote from the guts—further stimulated in many cases by starvation and abject living in the midst of Western affluence—not the more cerebral writing of the academic. Examples of such works, those pre-dating psychogeography but including examples of its style, include Jack London's *The People of the Abyss* (1903, observations on the "underworld" of London's East End); Stephen Graham's *New York Nights* (1927) and *London Nights* (1929), George Orwell's *Down and Out in Paris and London* (1933), Henry Miller's *Tropic of Cancer* (1934), Blaise Cendrars' *The Astonished Man* (1945), Jean-Paul Clébert's *Paris Vagabond* (1952), Jim Phelan's *Tramping the Toby* (1955); not to mention Jean Genet's *The Thief's Journal* (1949) and Violette Leduc's autobiographical works from 1946 onwards. The latter two writers were drawn together by shared experiences: both were illegitimate (Genet from a prostitute and Leduc from a servant girl), both were involved in petty criminality and vagabondage from an early age, and both were openly homosexual at a time when same-sex relationships were criminalized; all of which vividly informed their writing bringing them to the attention and friendship of existentialist philosophers of the period such as Jean-Paul Sartre and Simone de Beauvoir (herself a committed walker of both natural and urban landscapes[5]), both of whom did much to promote their work.

---

[5] See Abbs, Annabel., *Wind Swept: why women walk*, London: Two Roads Books, 2021

The aforementioned book by Jean-Paul Clébert, *Paris Vagabond*, has been credited by Lucy (formally Luc) Sante in her book *The Other Paris* (2015) as one of the inspirations for the psychogeography movement as conceived by Guy Debord in his 1955 journal article. Sante notes that Clébert's own *dérive* walking "beggared" that of the Lettrists, which, as recounted in the November 1956 issue of the Belgian Surrealist journal *Les Lèvres Nues*, she describes as "pretty small beer." The following passages from *Paris Vagabond* evidence why Sante should make such a statement as well as clearly marking out the urban vagabond from the general public. In the first passage, Clébert (2016, p. 50) also reinforces the distinction between the tramp writer and the literary vagabond in his own terms: 'vagabond poet' and 'poet vagabond':

> The revelation of the life of a city is not accessible to the public but reserved for initiates, for a very few poets and very many vagabonds. Each individual's perception of that life depends on their temperament and emotional resources, on their particular vision, be it deadened, disgusted, or razor sharp. The city is inexhaustible. And to master it one must indeed be either a vagabond poet or a poet vagabond.

In terms of what it is that fuels the urban vagabond's interest, in his description below of exploring Paris, Clébert (2016, p. 45) precisely mirrors Stephen Graham's accounts above of exploring London:

> Leisurely strolls quite obviously (and fortunately) [are] unknown to the tourist trade, for there is nothing to see on these routes except for poetry in the rough, which paying travellers would never appreciate: the poetry of masonry, cobbles, boundary stones, carriage entrances, dormer windows, tiled roofs, patches of grass, odd trees, dead ends, byways, blind alleys, inner courtyards, storage sheds for coal or building materials, wreckers' yards; the poetry of workshops, still vacant lots, bowling alleys, bistros-cum-refreshment stands; the poetry of colours but also of smells, a different smell for every doorway. Serpentine itineraries winding on endlessly, interminable itineraries open to anyone who knows how to wander and how to look, who has the nerve to go through portes-cochères, into workers' housing precincts, down private streets, who has the calmness of a guy at home everywhere.

Blaise Cendrars had been writing, and later movie making, since the first decade of the twentieth century, but the passage below was published in 1945, ten years before the label psychogeography was first employed. It provides one of the best examples that the practice and literary genre was already in practice, if not specifically identified as psychogeography. As Cendrars acknowledges, "It has always surprised me that so few modern writers, no matter how sensitive to the pathos of our era, have drawn their material from the suburbs." He acknowledges spending ten to twelve years "prowling" the area described below, "on foot, on horseback, or in a car." But as well as being a bohemian and a *flâneur*, Cendrars was also a country vagabond, on one occasion isolating himself in a disused barn for a year to write. This again questions just how helpful these terms are. His tramping and writing took place not only in his adopted home of Paris, as a child vagabond aged 15, he set out for, among other places, Russia, Persia, and China, later losing his right arm in the French Foreign Legion, and later still adding North and Latin America to his travels and work. But here is a sample of Cendrars' poetic prose about the Paris suburbs first published in 1945, which the Irish Times described as, "Dull as ditch-water, who but Cendras could make them more exciting than most travel writers have ever succeeded in making Rome?"

> The ring roads, known as La Petite and La Grande Ceinture, are a crown of thorns set in a double circlet on the emaciated brow of Paris. There are hospices in the waste lots planted with acacias as skinny as broom-handles, and housing estates among the muddy ploughed lands, fenced off with stakes and barbed wire, in the vicinity of the riverside factories that vomit black smoke and cinders and gulp down strings of coal-barges, which glide over the fetid and oily water into their overheated entrails; a house of retirement for old actors, lunatic asylums, orphanages, workhouses. Modern abattoirs, power stations, radio stations, airfields. Hundreds and hundreds of kilometres of railway sidings. Iron bridges, footbridges made of reinforced concrete, tens of thousands of arc-lamps, little all night bistros, hundreds of thousands of kilowatts, everything drenched in rain and every raindrop fouled with grease [...] It goes on raining. You flounder. The lowering sky, like a sponge soaked in gall, tamps down the Parisian landscape. It drips rust. Filth and refuse. Sparks fly across the high tension cables, a glow belches forth from the mouths of furnaces, the window-panes of workshops and operating theatres are tinged with a bluish glint, Flame colour, putrefaction, phosphorescence. There are will-o'-the-wisps that light up and are extinguished along the roads and by the quagmires. The tinkle of bicycle bells. Gasometers poison the atmosphere, the distilleries and the knackers' yard stink. It is a slow death and the furious yapping of the animal pound. '... One more thrust madam, and it's life.' In all the maternity hospitals they are being delivered by mass-production. One more thrust and everything cracks .... (Cendrars, 2004, p. 187)

Given the futility and pointlessness of categorizing someone like Cendrars into a precise societal or literary genre, and having considered the literary output of all those others in this chapter respectively labeled bohemian, *flâneur*, and psychogeographer (as well as sometimes tramping the open road), in conclusion, I will simply stay with the term 'urban vagabond' as the most helpful generic description of all the above writers. The next chapter will discuss another feature that marks the vagabond out from the rest of Nietzsche's 'human herd.'

Chapter 4

THE LONE AND LOFTY PERCH OF WORLD-HATING INTROSPECTION

The title of this chapter is borrowed from Timothy Bewes' book, *Cynicism and Postmodernity*, in which Bewes (1997, p. 171) describes the cynic's alienation from mainstream society as "an ascent into the lone and lofty perch of world-hating introspection." This alienation and cutting oneself off from the fundamental values of the society in which one lives is an attitude also summed up by Luis Navia (1998, p. 73) when he tells us that, "those who find the world something worthy of praise, or who congratulate themselves for having been born into the world, are either intellectually blind or morally perverse." Bewes (1997, p. 5) describes contemporary cynicism as "a strategic mode of thinking" which, in Peter Sloterdijk's words (1988, p. 5), "is the universally widespread way in which enlightened people see to it that they are not taken for suckers." Rickett's (1906, p. 6) own take on this aspect of vagabondage is described as follows in his Introduction:

> a passion for the Earth is not sufficient of itself to admit within the charmed circle of the Vagabond; for there is no marked restlessness about Mr. Meredith's genius, and he lacks what it seems to me is the third note of the genuine literary Vagabond—the note of aloofness, of personal detachment. This it is which separates the Vagabond from the generality of his fellows. No very prolonged scrutiny of the disposition of Thoreau, Jefferies, and Borrow is needed to reveal a pronounced shyness and reserve. Examine this trait more closely, and it will exhibit a certain emotional coldness towards the majority of men and women. No one can overlook the chill austerity that marks Thoreau's attitude in social converse. Borrow, again, was inaccessible to a degree, save to one or two intimates; even when discovered among congenial company, with the gipsies or with companions of the road like Isopel Berners, exhibiting, to me, a genial bleakness that is occasionally exasperating.

Later in the book, Rickett (1906, p. 111) notes the following admiration for those who reject conventional society:

> The Vagabond who withdraws himself to any extent from the life of his day, who declines to conform to many of its arbitrary conventions,

escapes much of the fret and tear, the heart-aching and the disillusionment that others share in. He retains a freshness, a simplicity, a joyfulness, not vouchsafed to those who stay at home and never wander beyond the prescribed limits. He exhibits an individuality which is more genuinely the legitimate expression of his temperament. It is not warped, crossed, suppressed, as many are.

Rickett provides several further examples of the vagabond's alienation from society. The first being from Maxim Gorky, whom he describes as "the Vagabond naked and unashamed" and Gorky's novels as "fervent defences of the Vagabond":

> I was born outside society, and for that reason I cannot take in a strong dose of its culture, without soon feeling forced to get outside it again, to wipe away the infinite complications, the sickly refinements, of that kind of existence. I like either to go about in the meanest streets of towns, because, though everything there is dirty, it is all simple and sincere; or else to wander about in the high roads and across the fields, because that is always interesting; it refreshes one morally, and needs no more than a pair of good legs to carry one. (Gorky cited in Rickett, 1906, p. 11)

In Rickett's chapter on Walt Whitman, we are presented with another insight into the vagabond writer's alienation from the pretensions of civilization. Rickett (1906, p. 170) describes Whitman as a modern-day Diogenes, striding, "stark naked among our academies of learning. A strange, uncouth, surprising figure, it is impossible to ignore him however much he may shock our susceptibilities." As with the Cynic's, Whitman's diatribe against society's evils is not preaching or evangelical, he is not proposing an alternative society, "this is done in no doctrinaire spirit", but rather as a way of being true to himself and what he regards as the "powerful uneducated person". In Thomas de Quincey, Rickett finds a man of a conservative turn of mind with an ingrained respect for the conventions of life, yet temperamentally a restless Vagabond with a total disregard for the amenities of civilization, asking only to live out his own dream life:

> Dealing with him as a writer, you found a shrewd, if wayward critic, with no little of "John Bull" in his composition. Deal with him as a man, you found a bright, kindly, nervous little man in a chronic state of shabbiness, eluding the attention of friends so far as possible, and wandering about town and country as if he had nothing in common with the rest of mankind. His Vagabondage is shown best in his purely

imaginative work, and in the autobiographical sketches. (Rickett, 1906, p. 46)

ESCAPE FROM THE HUMAN HERD

As already noted, the vagabond's alienation from "the rest of mankind" is an irresistible force brought on by a realization that the 'civilized' world is governed by a morality and sentimentality the vagabond sees as a folly to which he will not succumb. That even a vagabond such as de Quincey, grounded as he was in conventional society, could not resist this feeling of alienation is a powerful testimony to the power of its force. Nietzsche, while sharing this same view of the world, uses alienation in a different sense. In his case, it is the greater mass of humanity, his 'human herd,' who are alienated by sacrificing their own individual personality and integrity to the anonymous, coercive whole. A process, aided by 'education', where individual will is ultimately given over to the collective will of the wider group. In this sense, the vagabond resists alienating him or herself from their own integrity in the face of powerful forces to conform to the common will of the society in which they live. The price is to be banished to the margins of mainstream society, the prize is to be free from shackles that bind one to it. Rickett (1906, pp. 159-160) himself acknowledges the negative side of this herding instinct when he suggests that most of us would benefit from spending time alone with nature rather than herded together with the rest of our species:

> We herd together so much—some unhappily by necessity, some by choice, that it would be a refreshing thing, and a wholesome thing, for most of us to be alone, more often face to face with the primal forces of Nature.

The vagabond spirit, then, is one that defies society's pressure to conform because the vagabond cannot help but see that civilization is bankrupt of any moral purpose—for them, at least. A moral vacuum reinforced by humans' desperate need, and constant attempts, to make the world a better place, yet always failing and often in the most spectacular way. And one of the ways that humans have devised to trick themselves into believing in their own cleverness and superiority in the animal kingdom, is to replace the vacuum of ideas with idealist rhetoric. The use of 'soundbites' has reached epidemic proportions in the age of mass, electronic communication, and this, in turn, has only amplified the hollowness of the human civilizing project. In his collection of essays, *Virginibus Puerisque,* Robert Louis Stevenson was acutely aware of this aspect of human behavior when he noted, almost a century and a half ago, how the mass of society communicate through soundbites rather than serious argument:

To have a catchword in your mouth is not the same thing as to hold an opinion; still less is it the same thing as to have made one for yourself. There are too many of these catchwords in the world for people to rap out upon you like an oath by way of an argument. They have a currency as intellectual counters, and many respectable persons pay their way with nothing else. (R.L. Stephenson cited in Rickett, 1906, p. 131)

THE VAGABOND'S VULNERABILITY

But then, the ancient Cynics were already making similar observations over 2000 years ago. Diogenes' very raison d'être was to deface the false currency of human being's rhetoric, "I was exiled for literally 'altering the currency'; my philosophy teaches men to 'alter the currency' in another sense. Let us strike out of circulation false standards and values of all kinds" (cited in Dudley, 1937, p. 22). I have previously used the example of Diogenes' reported meeting with Alexander (the Great) to identify the role of the *parrhesiast*: those who feel compelled to speak the truth—their truth—even at the risk of harm to themselves:

The *parrhesiast* speaks the truth because it is the truth, and, as in the case of Alexander, not always the truth that people wish to hear. It is the courage to say something which endangers the speaker that distinguishes the *parrhesiast* from those like the rhetorician who use discourse to seduce. (Cutler, 2005, p. 29)

As with the risks of taking the stance of the *parrhesiast*, the vagabond's alienation from wider society, the lone and lofty stance described by Bewes, comes at a cost. It is not a comfortable or easy position to take, as Thoreau (cited in Rickett, 1906, p. 11) noted when he acknowledged that, "the Vagabond loses as well as gains by his deliberate withdrawal from the world." Indeed, Bewes' cynical vagabond feels envy for the 'metaphysically innocent,' those who appear unconcerned at the world's imperfections and even appear to prosper on account of their freedom from such intellectual preoccupations. The vagabond may even feel handicapped and tortured by his or her alienation from the rest of the human herd. And so in this sense, the vagabond's alienation is not a position of superiority, certainly, they do not scorn their fellow humans, but rather feel dismay that humans should and could have made a better job of their place on earth, but haven't.

As the modern-day vagabond philosopher, Raymond Federman (2000, p. 126), observed, "true cynics are often the kindest people, for they see the hollowness of life, and from the realization of that hollowness is generated a kind of cosmic pity". In the vagabond, this kindness does not so much manifest itself on an individual level but, as Federman acknowledges, extends to humankind as a whole. As Rickett (1906, p. 190) notes: "A man may exhibit kindliness and tenderness towards his fellow creatures without showing any deep personal attachment."

In his partly autobiographical, third-person narrative *Jarnegan*, tramp writer Jim Tully reinforces that the vagabond does not claim to know better than those he alienates himself from and certainly, like the Cynic, does not seek to persuade them to his own view of the world. His cynicism is more of a positive response to the noise of those who *do* offer truth and meaning, identifying himself as a "cynical realist" in the process:

> A man of no isms, he was tolerant of everything that did not touch his life. He knew nothing of nations or their rulers. He had never voted. Neither had he any theories about life. A cynical realist, he fought against the sentimentality that was his Irish inheritance. At times, in his cups, he ended by being that most ironical of humans—a sentimental cynic. (Tully, 1926, p. 131)

There is no contradiction here in being a sentimental cynic. This is to misunderstand the true nature of cynicism, which, in spite of its acerbic and forthright nature, is often misinterpreted as contemptuous and sneering, even nihilistic. On the contrary, it can often be positive, idealistic, even sentimental. As noted above, the true soul of the vagabond or Cynic is simply to mourn the fact that human beings have made a mess of the world they inhabit and act so foully towards one and another.

Neither is there a contradiction when Tully says he hasn't "any theories about life." He is not referring here to his personal philosophy, but to the grand narratives that feed the march of progress yet always fall short of delivering human happiness. Our cynical vagabond knows that the human project is fundamentally flawed, and so any theories are confined to maintaining one's integrity against what he or she views as a hostile world. Both the vagabond and cynic's mission, if they have one at all, is to maximize their own life here on earth rather than seek to change or control the world around them—which, in any case, they know to be capricious, chaotic, and *beyond* human control. In order to achieve contentment, as well as minimizing our dependence on material possessions, we are urged to rely on our own natural instincts rather than listening to the daily babble of egotistical buffoons.

It is important to emphasize again that, for the most part, the vagabond writers discussed in this text did not seek to persuade others to their point of view. These are not evangelical movements and the individuals concerned, while sharing many views and attitudes about the world, do not identify with each other as a tribe. As Rickett (1906, p. 103) further notes:

> The Vagabond has his philosophy of life no less than the moralist, though as a rule he is content to let it lie implicit in his writings, and is not anxious to turn it into a gospel. But he did not always realize the difference between moral characteristics and temperamental peculiarities, and many of his admirers have done him ill service by trying to make of his very Vagabondage (admirable enough in its way) a rule of faith for all and sundry.

THE VAGABOND'S RESPONSE TO MAINSTREAM SOCIETY'S VIEW OF THEM

As much as the vagabond pours scorn on mainstream civilization, many of society's regular citizens can be equally dismissive, even hostile, toward the vagabond. This view is described below in George Orwell's (2021, p. 200) defense of the tramp, even though he is talking about the tramp in general rather than about the tramp writer or literary vagabond:

> These prejudices are rooted in the idea that every tramp, ipso facto, is a blackguard. ... consequently, there exists in our minds a sort of ideal or typical tramp—a repulsive, rather dangerous creature, who would rather die than work or wash, and wants nothing but to beg, drink, and rob hen-houses. This tramp-monster is no truer to life than the sinister Chinaman of the magazine stories, but it is very hard to get rid of. The very word 'tramp' evokes his image. And the belief in him obscures the real questions of vagrancy.

The myth that wider society has viewed the vagabond as a threat to civilized society is also challenged by Bart Kennedy in his book *A Tramp's Philosophy* (1908, p. 16) when he says:

> He [the tramp] knows that trouble will come to this civilisation, but not from men like him. It will come from the idiot slaves whose ideal is to be as well off as their masters. ... He is the pioneer of a finer and calmer life. He wanders along, a real philosopher.

Kennedy's notion of a slave mentality that maintains the status quo of civilization based on a drive for a share of the wealth and possessions of the slave masters is further articulated by Thoreau (cited in Belloc, 1911, p. 87):

I rejoice that horses and steers have to be broken before they can be made the slaves of men, and that men themselves have some wild oats still left to sow before they become submissive members of society. Undoubtedly, all men are not equally fit subjects for civilisation; and because the majority, like dogs and sheep, are tame by inherited disposition, this is no reason why the others should have their natures broken that they may be reduced to the same level.

The passages above shift conventional society's view of the vagabond as a lower form of the human species by using the slave metaphor to elevate the vagabond as having greater intelligence and courage than the rest of the human herd; a view that allows the vagabond philosopher to maintain their freedom from what they view as the tyrannies of civilization, but at the same time, unless a 'successful' writer, yet remaining vulnerable and dispossessed from the society they denounce. One of the ways the vagabond survives being marginalized in the community into which they were born is to adopt the entire planet as their home.

COSMOPOLITANISM

To an identifiable tribe, they may not belong, but when necessity presents itself, the vagabond will be open to and readily borrow from any other ethnic, religious or cultural group that suits their needs. They are, first and foremost, individuals who do not recognize political borders or man-made regulations and customs. As Nietzsche (1909, p. 25) observed, "It is so provincial to bind oneself to views which are no longer binding a couple of hundred miles away." There is an understanding among most vagabonds that the world was not created for the benefit of humans alone, and hence, man-made constructs are rejected in favor of an alliance with the entire natural world. I first described this theme in my book on Cynicism when I noted that the Cynics' ideal republic was one without boundaries or social distinctions. It was not restricted to a geographical place, nor to a racial or ethnic group, nor to historical or cultural traditions. For Diogenes, allegiance to a city or nation was a manifestation of sheer stupidity (Navia, 1996, p. 101). Hence the description of Cynics in the Introduction to this book as, "citizens of the world, or cosmos: the first cosmopolitans".

Not only did the Cynics reject ties of statehood and patriotism, maintaining that the wise person does not fight for their country (Dudley, 1937, p. 105), but we are told by Farrand Sayre (1938, p. 13), who maintains the tradition for defaming the Cynics, that they broke ties of family, which in Diogenes case included suggesting that there should be no gratitude to one's parents for being born as we were simply creatures generated by nature. Such an attitude is acknowledged by Thoreau (cited in Belloc, 1911, pp. 53-54) as a necessary requirement to become a true vagabond:

> If you are ready to leave father and mother, and brother and sister, and wife and child and friends, and never see them again—if you have paid your debts, and made your will, and settled all your affairs, and are a free man, then you are ready for a walk.

And so, the epithet cosmopolite is equally applicable to the modern vagabond and for the same reason as that credited to the ancient Cynics. Hazlitt (cited in Belloc, 1911, p. 32) reminds us of the human arrogance in believing that the world is the one we have mapped out on charts:

> The world in our conceit of it is not much bigger than a nutshell. It is not one prospect expanded into another, county joined to county, kingdom to kingdom, land to seas, making an image voluminous and vast; the mind can form no larger idea of space than the eye can take in at a single glance. The rest is a name written in a map, a calculation of arithmetic.

HOW THE VAGABOND REGARDS THEMSELVES

To be a cosmopolite, though, is not a badge one wears. As already acknowledged, the vagabond does not identify with others of their kind in any formal sense, quite the reverse, it is about remaining true to one's own idiosyncratic nature. With some notable literary exceptions, such as Leon Ray Livingston's vigorous branding of his self-published works, the vagabond does not seek recognition for their unconventional way of being in the world. Rickett also warns us we must beware of sentimentalizing the vagabond and presenting him as an ideal figure. "It is well," he says, "for the Vagabond to be in the minority," and acknowledges that, for the most part, they have managed to remain under the radar in terms of their personal philosophies when he acknowledges that, "Thoreau is one of the few Vagabonds whom his admirers have tried to canonize." And, as though to reinforce the vagabond as an individual rather than a representative of a wider movement and credit them with virtues they never had, he notes the following:

> Not content with the striking qualities which the Vagabond naturally exhibits, some of his admirers cannot rest without dragging in other qualities to which he has no claim. Why try to prove that Thoreau was really a most sociable character, that Whitman was the profoundest philosopher of his day, that Jefferies was—deep down—a conventionally religious man? Why, oh why, may we not leave them in their pleasant

wildness without trying to make out that they were the best company in the world for five-o'clock teas and chapel meetings? (Rickett, 1906, p. 112)

Yet, as much as the vagabond may wish to remain anonymous and under the radar, there inevitably are those like myself who will become obsessed with identifying an underlying philosophy which clearly exists within the wild and unconventional lives of the vagabond writer, even if a simple and existential one:

> Approve it or reject it, however, as we may, 'tis a philosophy that can claim many and diverse adherents, for it is no dusty formula of academic thought, but a message of the sunshine and the winds. Talk of suffering and death to the Vagabond, and he will reply as did Petulengro, 'Life is sweet, brother.' Not that he ignores other matters, but it is sufficient for him that "life is sweet." And after all he speaks as to what he has known. (Rickett, 1906, p. 114)

THE VAGABOND'S RELATIONSHIP TO SOCIETY AT LARGE

The vagabond's relationship to society and societal groups is best described by Jeff Ferrell (2018, pp. 14-15), who, while acknowledging that most vagabonds are entirely social animals and enjoy human company, explains that, "drifting [Ferrell's term for vagabondage as described in this text] becomes an ongoing exercise in autonomy.":

> torn lose from the everyday structures and strictures of a sedentary existence, drifters take charge of their lives in ways that no settled homeowner or successful community stalwart can understand—or endure. [...] drifters' gritty escapes from the social order are seen to position them above and beyond it ...

Ferrell further notes (2018, pp. 45 and 47) how legal and political authority's actions to control the threat they regard vagabonds pose to social stability further reinforce the vagabonds' alienation from that society.

> Drift also invokes multiple dimensions and multiple moments of *transgression*. Transgression suggests a crossing over, a breaching of boundaries established by law and custom, map or morality. [...] The drifter exists as a perpetual outsider—outside the boundaries of home country, outside the conventional labour market, outside the protection of legal citizenship. ... A serial transgressor by law or by choice, the drifter is able to see—forced to see—the order of things from the other side.

If the vagabond is part of a community at all, Ferrell notes, such communities are decidedly unstable, "a volatile mix of on-the-fly individuals who share spaces and agendas that can evaporate on the spot." Yes, the vagabond can enjoy good times and tolerate difficult experiences with his fellow humans, but rather than nurture these friendships long-term, he suddenly disappears without explanation or farewell. In this sense, Ferrell continues, the world of the vagabond resembles a loosely shifting social web, "the scattered beads for a necklace that never quite gets strung, a world defined neither by isolated individuals nor by stable social groupings but by some amorphous space in between" (Ferrell, 2018, pp. 18-19).

Chapter 5

PETER PAN SYNDROME

These more eager, more adventurous spirits express for us the holiday mood of life. For they are young at heart, inasmuch as they have lived in the sunshine, and breathed in the fresh, untainted air. They have indeed scattered 'a new roughness and gladness' among men and women, for they have spoken to us of the simple magic of the Earth.

Arthur Rickett (1906, p. 11)

From the mind of childhood there is more history and more philosophy to be fished up than from all the printed volumes in a library. The child is conscious of an interest, not in literature but in life.

R. L. Stevenson (2022, p. 264)

EDUCATION -v- WISDOM

Rickett's observation that the vagabond is "young at heart" requires further analysis. A common theme in tramp literature is that the vagabond never loses their youthful innocence and has not been corrupted by the process of 'education.' Jim Phelan has described the tramp as "a lost child," Stephen Graham as "the boy who never grows old," Morley Roberts declares, "my youth is not ended," and Trader Horn is described as writing with the "clarity of a precocious child," and Rickett notes the popular characterization of Robert Louis Stevenson as "the eternal boy."

Could it be that when the tramp or vagabond turns their back on the tyranny of man-made rules and responsibilities and heads for the horizon, they are engaged in no more than a desperate attempt to hang on to the innocence of childhood? As Nietzsche (1909, p. 40) observed, there is something that the child sees and hears that others do not, and that "something" is the most important thing of all. Morley Roberts' *Tramp's Notebook* was published four years after Nietzsche's death, and so it is entirely possible that he was influenced by that philosopher's belief that real education is a far cry from the art of passing examinations, which, as Nietzsche (1909, pp. 173-174) claimed, "produce merely the savant or the official or the businessman."

Roberts relates how, aged 18, he exchanged his university education at Owens College, Manchester (where he met and befriended the writer George Gissing) for what he described as his "new university," four months working his passage on the 1,600-ton sailing ship Hydrabad bound for Melbourne. His journey on board ship was his first introduction to "world realities as distinct from the preliminary brutalities of school" and gave him an authentic view of the world as opposed to, "the substitutes for vision favoured by ... schoolmasters, professors, and good parents. How any child survives without losing his eyesight altogether is now a marvel to me." Those who survive at all, he says, retain only a dim vision that permits them to "wallow amongst imitations." His real professors, he says, were the crew on board the ship, and they taught him the art of seeing things the way they truly are (Roberts, 1904, pp. 53-54).

Roberts exposes an attitude toward formal education that is shared by many other writers cited in this book, that strong desire to avoid civilizing processes and hang on to the childlike innocence and illusions that those who do submit to "growing-up" relinquish. So if there is something childlike about the compulsion to reject the perceived wisdom of others, as Roberts freely admits he does, the term 'childlike' should not be viewed here in its pejorative sense. Along with both Phelan and Graham, Roberts believed that the world is a poorer place for having abandoned "old-fashioned habits of thought" and has allowed scientists to strip it of its magic. For Roberts (1904, p. 52), education suppresses true knowledge, and he describes his teachers as his jailers, whose only interest was the acquisition of knowledge for its own sake and the passing of examinations:

> The opinion is rooted deep in many minds that to surrender one's wings, to clip one's claws, to put a cork in one's raptorial beak, and masquerade in a commercial barnyard, is to be a very fine fowl indeed.

In Thoreau's diatribe against knowledge in his essay 'Walking', he describes knowledge as no more than, "a conceit that we know something, which robs us of the advantage of our actual ignorance?" Humans accumulate a myriad of facts, he says, but if and when they enter a period of serious reflection about life, they go to grass like a horse and leave all their harnesses behind in the stable. From this observation, Thoreau urges, "Go to grass. You have eaten hay long enough." Thoreau (cited in Belloc, 1911, pp. 92-93) sums up his argument by promoting ignorance as a virtue:

> A man's ignorance sometimes is not only useful, but beautiful,—while his knowledge, so called, is oftentimes worse than useless, besides being ugly. Which is the best man to deal with—he who knows nothing about a subject, and, what is extremely rare, knows that he knows nothing, or he who really knows something about it, but thinks that he knows all?

And so, if the acquisition of knowledge as presented by academic qualifications does not demonstrate wisdom, how then do we measure it? The following lines from Walt Whitman's poem *Song of the Open Road* (cited in Belloc, 1911, p. 148) provide us with a concise definition:

> Here is the test of wisdom,
>
> Wisdom is not finally tested in schools,
>
> Wisdom cannot be pass'd from one having it to another not having it,
>
> Wisdom is of the soul, is not susceptible of proof, is its own proof,
>
> Applies to all stages and objects and qualities and is content,
>
> Is the certainty of the reality and immortality of things, and the excellence of things;
>
> ...
>
> Now I re-examine philosophies and religions,
>
> They may prove well in lecture-rooms, yet not prove at all under the spacious clouds and along the landscape and flowing currents.

In the following passage, R. L. Stevenson (1905, p. 63) provides a portrait of those who have surrendered their ignorance and youthful innocence to an orthodox education and the world of commerce:

> His eyes were sealed by a cheap, school-book materialism. He could see nothing in the world but money and steam-engines. He did not know what you meant by the word happiness. He had forgotten the simple emotions of childhood, and perhaps never encountered the delights of youth. He believed in production, that useful figment of economy, as if it had been real like laughter ...

This theme of being socialized into conformity is repeated in Stevenson's travelogue *An Inland Voyage* (1904, p. 20) when he meets up with a group of enthusiastic youngsters at a Brussels boathouse where they helped him berth his canoe:

> The nightmare illusion of middle age, the bear's hug of custom gradually squeezing the life out of a man's soul, had not yet begun for these happy starred young Belgians. ... To know what you prefer, instead of humbly saying Amen to what the world tells you you ought to prefer, is to have kept your soul alive. ... He may be a man, in short, acting on his own

instincts, keeping in his own shape that God made him in; and not a mere crank in the social engine-house, welded on principles that he does not understand, and for purposes that he does not care for.

Robert Walser (1992, pp. 55-56 and 63) made similar observations to Stevenson when he came upon a group of children playing on one of his own walks.

Young boys and girls race around in the sunlight, free and unrestrained. 'Let them be unrestrained as they are,' I mused. 'Age one day will terrify and bridal them. Only too soon alas!' [...] Children are heavenly because they are always in a land of heaven. When they grow older and grow up, their heaven vanishes and then they fall out of their childishness into the dry calculating manner and tedious perception of adults.

And Bart Kennedy (1908, pp. 255-256) summarises all these arguments in his book, *A Tramp's Philosophy*, when he says that:

... the fact is that men get more stupid as they grow older. The human being starts with a good bright mind. As everyone knows, children are famous for their straight and apt and acute way of viewing things. But the child's mind is soon, alas! dulled by the process that is called education. Schools and colleges and other brain-benumbing institutions kill the mother-wit that the human began with.

Why, then, does the vagabond prefer an education outside of orthodox learning establishments like schools and universities. As with the ancient Cynics, the modern vagabond only trusts what is experienced directly through their own senses. Unlike the academic philosopher, the vagabond philosopher is not interested in discovering why or how something is because such knowledge would destroy the magic and exotic nature of the phenomena or experience—rendering it mundane. Why should the vagabond care about the scientific discovery of how many sub-atomic neutrinos are emitted by the sun, it is enough simply to bask in its warmth; of course, we find using a computer more convenient than writing on papyrus, but are our lives made any happier as a result? Is our writing any more potent? Like the Cynics then, the vagabond philosopher *lives* their philosophy rather than preaching it, as observed below by Blaise Cendrars (2004, pp. 198-199):

I am not an erudite man. I distrust references which, nine time out of ten, turn out to be false or inexact when you check them, and are erroneous or misinterpreted in the accompanying commentaries so as to put forward or defend a theory, not to mention the rivalries of the various schools, and the vanity of the various personalities involved [...] I do not know how scholars work. For myself, I have to see things with my own eyes, touch them with my fingers, in order to understand and love them, and mingle myself with them in thought and reinvent them to animate them and make them live again and again. Without the gift of creation, science is a dead letter.

A theme common to all these writers is the stupidity of adults absorbed through a process of maturation; not acquiring wisdom, but rather losing it through false learning. Humans are the most arrogant of animals, oblivious to the fact that in their attempts to understand the world and shape it to their will, they instead create the very chaos and disorder that they seek to control. At the core of the vagabond's determination not to participate in the conceit that afflicts so many of their fellow humans is a search for a simpler, more meaningful life.

THE IMPULSE AND INQUISITIVENESS OF CHILDHOOD

Rickett (1906, p. 51) claims that a characteristic attitude of the vagabond is an eager and insatiable curiosity towards life, "a good deal of the child's eagerness to know how a thing happened, and who this is, and what that is." He talks about the impulse that gave Borrow his zest for travel in other countries and "the impulse that sent De Quincey wandering over the various roads of intellectual and emotional inquiry." And so, the natural inquisitiveness of childhood is also one of the driving forces behind wanderlust. But to return to the nature of childhood itself, when Rickett opens his chapter on George Borrow, he asks the question of why we eagerly demand a story of our elders as soon as we can toddle and why "once upon a time" can achieve what moral strictures are powerless to effect?

> It is because to most of us the world of imagination is the world that matters. We live in the "might be's" and "peradventures." Fate may have cast our lot in prosaic places; have predetermined our lives on humdrum lines; but it cannot touch our dreams. ... Our bodies may traverse the same dismal streets day after day; but our minds rove luxuriantly through all the kingdoms of the earth. [...] But there are dreams by sunlight and visions at noonday also. Such dreams thrill us in another but no less unmistakable way, especially when the dreamer is a Scott, a William Morris, a Borrow. (1906, p. 58)

Dreamers like Borrow, Rickett suggests, "are not content to see visions and dream dreams, their bodies must participate no less than their minds." And so, back to wanderlust again; the hardships and privations chronicled in the child tramp adventures presented below, did not deter the vagabond from setting forth in quest of the unknown. It is precisely the rare and the unexpected that drive their adventures and satisfy their desires. Stephen Graham (1926, p. 47) acknowledges this when he writes, "the desire to know what is beyond the next turning of the road ... the born wanderer is always expecting to come on something very wonderful—beyond the horizon's rim." Graham was the first to acknowledge that the joys of wandering are balanced by the pains, but that his own desire to wander was incurable from childhood. When taken to places he had never been before as a child, Graham (1926, p. 47) refers to the experience as being a child of the "wander-thrill."

> I remember from the age of nine a barefoot walk with my mother along the Lincolnshire sands from Sutton to Skegness, and the romantic and strange sights on the way. What did we not build out of that adventure?

Below, Rickett (1906, pp. 102-103) provides a further explanation for the vagabond writer's childlike behavior:

> Every Vagabond swaggers because he is an egotist more or less, and relishes keenly the life he has mapped out for himself. But the swagger is of the harmless kind; it is not really offensive; it is a sort of childish exuberance that plays over the surface of his mind, without injuring it, the harmless vanity of one who having escaped from the schoolhouse of convention congratulates himself on his good luck.

THE ADULT VAGABOND'S AFFINITY WITH CHILDREN

What attracts us most in children is naturalness and simplicity. We note in them the frank predominance of the instinctive life, and they charm us in many ways just as young animals do.

Henry D. Thoreau (cited in Rickett, 1906, p. 110)

Yet Thoreau parts company with other vagabond writers, in refusing to employ the term 'innocent' to describe children, "The innocence and purity of children is a middle-class convention," in reality, he says, they are "brought up in a morbidly sentimental atmosphere that makes of them too quickly little prigs or little hypocrites." But for the purposes of this book, I use the term 'childhood innocence' as other vagabond writers have done, to refer to its more general meaning as the "naturalness and simplicity" Thoreau makes in his quote above. The Oxford University Press (2023) definition of 'childhood innocence' also includes, "not yet spoiled by mundane affairs", an important element of the discussion that follows.

Rickett maintains that it is these natural and instinctive qualities, "children who have the freshness and wildness of the woods about them", that the vagabond relates to and seeks to emulate in their own life, in turn rejecting the civilized conventions adopted by their more orthodox contemporaries. Tramp writer Jim Phelan's (1955, p. 90) approach to the Peter Pan analogy is that, "a vagabond is really a lost child, who sometimes finds his mother—his mother being represented by a thousand women, in a thousand different towns." The theme of Phelan's "lost children," whether searching for their home or their mothers, is evident from the passage below from *Tramping the Toby*, where he shares Graham's loss of a bygone age when old-fashioned wisdom prevailed; the loss of childhood innocence clearly having parallels with the deprivation of earthly simplicity:

> people who live in the wild regions, shepherds and explorers and vagabonds, those who travel the lonely roads and know the dark silent places of the earth—those people have the old-fashioned habits of thought, and they believe in many things which the townspeople would call mere superstition ... and old fashioned and unscientific belief. (1955, p. 81)

Morley Roberts (1904, p. 59) also admits to a desire for perpetual youth when he states in his work *A Tramp's Note-Book* that, "without illusion one cannot write" and that (and herein lies a perfectly expressed manifesto for the life of the professional tramp):

> When the Queen of Illusion illudes no more youth is over.' [...] To do a little useful work (even though the useful may be a thousandth part of the useless) is the end of living. The only illusion worth keeping is that anything can be useful. So far my youth is not ended.

If childish curiosity goes hand-in-hand with childish innocence, it also embraces a particular wisdom. For the vagabond philosopher, 'civilization' represents the downfall of humanity, not its triumph, and in the following passage from Stephen Graham's, *A Tramp's Sketches* (1913, p. 209), we have the ultimate thesis on the wisdom of youth:

> Old age, old age; I was an old, bearded, heavy-going, wrinkled tramp, leaning on a stout stick; my grey hairs blew about my old red ears in wisps. I stopped all passers-by upon the road, and chuckled over old jokes or detained them with garrulity. But no, not old; nor will the tramp

ever be old, for he has in his bosom that by virtue of which, even in old age, he remains a boy. There is in him, like the spring buds among the withered leaves of autumn, one never-dying fountain of youth. He is the boy who never grows old.

And so, do not underestimate the childish simplicity of the vagabond philosopher's character for behind it lurks a superior intellect. This again raises the question of who the *real* outcasts from humanity are; a theme picked up firstly by Bart Kennedy in his book *Sailor Tramp* (1902, p. 107) and secondly by Stephen Graham in *A Tramp's Sketches* (1913, p. 239). Both of these vagabond philosophers leave warnings for those who dismiss the tramp and hold him or her in contempt:

> Tramps and outcasts. Be easy with them. For it may come to pass that they will be held up to honour as the brave rebels and pioneers, who guided men up the tortuous path of intelligence and happiness.

> [The tramp] is necessarily a masked figure; he wears the disguise of one who has escaped, and also of one who is a conspirator. ... He is the walking hermit, the world-forsaker, but he is above all things a rebel and a prophet, and he stands in very distinct relation to the life of his time.

ANECDOTES OF CHILD TRAMPING ADVENTURES

This chapter would not be complete without reference to some of the childhood adventures of tramp writers cited in the text. The stories that follow have been summarised from the biographies in my book *The Golden Age Of Vagabondage* (2020):

Leon Ray Livingston's father was French, his mother German, and by the age of eight, he could speak both these languages fluently in addition to English, to which he later added Spanish. At the age of eleven, a minor incident at school led to Livingston running away from home to join hundreds of other homeless children and hobos roaming across America: a river steamboat from San Francisco to Sacramento, stranded in the Nevada desert at Winnemucca, from there to Chicago, ending up in New Orleans on Christmas Day, 1883. On New Year's Day he was offered a job as a cabin boy on board a British schooner plying trade among the ports of Central America at $5 a day plus board. In Belize City he was employed as a bookkeeper in a lumber camp, a nine-day journey upriver, setting off sometime later to tramp the 220-mile journey to Guatemala City. From there, a 1,200-mile overland trek alone to Mexico City and in Albuquerque, he was arrested for vagrancy and locked up "in a dark and filthy cell." Livingston arrived in Lathrop, California, via Salt Lake City, exactly one year after he had run away from his parent's home, and only 97 miles from his destination, San Francisco. But instead of returning home, the now thirteen-year-old Livingston was offered a job as a waiter by the steward of a German steamer bound for Hamburg. At the age of fifteen, Livingstone embarked on an even more remarkable journey that nearly lost him his life, and did lose the life of his traveling companion. It involved navigating the Amazon River and tributaries for 5,000 miles. After arriving in Venezuela following a lone trek through Mexico and Panama, he hitched up with another child tramp where, with the help of two burros, they traveled the 1,250 miles via Colombia and Ecuador across the Andean mountain peaks until eventually reaching the navigable source of the Amazon tributary, the Rio Napo. There, they swapped their burros for a canoe—the rest of the story makes the trip so far sound like a jaunt.

Jack Everson, also from a comfortable middle-class family, suffered his first arrest, aged ten, for undertaking a mile-long swim to Government Pier, Chicago, in the nude. This also earned him a beating from his father, who had to pay the $10 fine. An experienced petty criminal by the age of eleven, Everson was also experienced in the sexual arts after being befriended by a prostitute who offered him her services for free. Still aged eleven, and after a particularly vicious beating from his father for being accused (falsely, he claims) of stealing a penknife from another boy, Everson jumped a train heading for New York with an older boy. Getting off the train when it stopped after some 40 miles, the pair were persuaded by two seasoned tramps to split up and accompany them separately, the one pair to California, with Everson and the other tramp going to New York. As luck would have it, Everson's jocker, "Michigan Curly," turned out to be kindness personified, and the two became close friends for many years. Curly completed Everson's education in the arts of begging, burglary and how to avoid jail. But Everson did not avoid jail and, by the age of fourteen, was jailed for a second time (the first was for peddling fake jewelry), this time for possession of a stolen Colt .45 revolver that had been among some other items Everson agreed to peddle for a tramp who failed to tell him the gun had been stolen. At the age of 16, following his father's death from a ruptured aneurism and ignoring pleas from his mother to continue with his education, Everson boarded a ship to work his passage to Australia via Honolulu. And so his adventures continued.

Jack London's childhood (revolving around both tramping and alcohol) are best evidenced in his autobiography *The Road*, and his exposition on his love/hate relationship with alcohol in *John Barleycorn* (possibly the best philosophical treatise on the subject ever written). London first got drunk at the age of five after being asked, one hot summer day, to carry a pail of beer to his father, who was plowing a field half a mile away. On the second occasion, at the age of seven, London got drunk on red wine in the company of some older children and adults. He was bullied into drinking a glass of wine, only to shock those around him by downing several more without showing any ill effects until, that is, collapsing unconscious in a ditch on his way home and experiencing the most terrible nightmares for several days following. On eventually emerging from his delirium, London recalled his mother's voice declaring, "But the child's brain. He will lose his reason." Initially, he found both beer and wine unpleasant, both in their taste and effect: "very clear was my resolution never to touch liquor again. No mad dog was ever more afraid of water than was I of alcohol." London's wanderlust was further fuelled by drinking in the saloons around San Fransisco Bay and London became a sailor tramp before jumping trains. By the age of 15 he had his own sloop and became the most notorious oyster pirate in the Bay. The incident that earned him his spurs occurred when a seasoned oyster pirate, French Frank, tried to run him down with his schooner. London stood coolly on the deck, a cocked double-barrelled shotgun in his hands and held his sloop on course with his feet, forcing French Frank to alter course to avoid a collision. Aged 16 he jumped a train for the first time. One of a group of a dozen road kids heading out of Sacramento to cross the Rocky Mountains on a Central Pacific overland train. There was only one other "first-timer" attempting to board the train with London that day, but he never made it. He stumbled on boarding the train, and both his legs were amputated by the wheels.

At the age of four, Jim Phelan, fuelled by the images of stories from both his mother and father, and drawn by the sights and sounds of Dublin and the countryside beyond, embarked on his first tramping adventure. He had planned for three days, with the penny his mother gave him for sweets on his way to school, to follow the railway line to Tipperary, a distance of over a hundred miles. So good was Phelan at spinning a line of guff that he managed to fool two police officers who questioned him on his journey, arriving in Tipperary days later to the astonishment and surprise of relatives. At the age of seven, anticipating a beating for knocking his sister helpless with a clothes-brush and some trouble over missing apples, Phelan grabbed a bottle of milk and part of a loaf of bread and headed off to the canal basin where he hid himself under a tarpaulin covering a barge until discovered by the barge-men the following day. He was handed over to a kindly priest who, after offering him food and a bed for the night, sent Phelan home by train with a letter to his parents. By the age of 13, Phelan had stowed away on a ship to Glasgow. Where he spent over a month learning to speak "Scotch." "To me Glasgow looked, smelt, and sounded like a dream town. Now this was a real foreign city at last. I could not understand one word of the speech. Heaven!"

Jim Christy is the contemporary vagabond whose life and adventures are the subject of my biography *A Vagabond Life* (2019). Christy's wanderlust is referred to in Chapter 1, but his first tramp at the age of 12 included a six-week hike on foot from his home in Southern Philadelphia to the Canadian border via New York, returning on foot after the start of the new school term and ending up in police custody for his trouble. He had told his parents that he did not want to accompany them that year on their regular summer vacation to Virginia, where Christy's maternal family lived, but that he was going to stay at the house of a school friend—as confirmed to Christy's mother by the other boy's inebriated mother. On trying to cross the Niagara Falls bridge to Canada, he met a seasoned tramp crossing in the other direction. An immediate bond of comradeship was struck up between the aging Russian Count and the child vagabond. Several more weeks were spent returning part of the way with the Count, and their many adventures are recorded in Christy's unpublished manuscript, *Reet, Petite and Gone*. The following Spring, Christy ran away again after reading a Sunday magazine supplement about the Beat Generation. He stayed with the beatniks in Philadelphia for six weeks before being arrested following a police raid on one of their hangouts. Christy was interrogated about whether he smoked marijuana, was a communist or a "pinko" and, when they discovered his age, whether he could help them pin a morals charge on the older beatniks. His third child tramp followed him, spotting an advert for a "roughie" in *Amusement Business* at a circus in Kokomo, Indiana; but not before spending 24 hours in Canton County Jail, Ohio, for hitchhiking on the Interstate and refusing to pay the fine. The full adventures of this trip are recorded in Christy's book *Jackpots* (2012).

Other such stories are plentiful, but this is not the place to record the tramp writers' biographical adventures. I simply present these examples here to illustrate how the wanderlust 'affliction' manifests itself in the child vagabond; behaviors that are often maintained into adulthood and, in turn, influenced the writing style that emerges from the vagabond literature cited in this book. Writing about the tramp writer Trader Horn, William McFee (Foreword in Horn, 2002, pp. 10-11) notes that what gives Horn's adult writing its particular quality is that it is written with the "clarity of a precocious child":

> When reading, our pleasure is derived in the first place from seeing the story-telling faculty, reduced to its simplest components, operating in full view of the reader. ... neither Dickens nor Dostoevsky ever cut so cleanly or so deep to the very quick of the poverty problem as does Mr. Horn ... we who write have to admit that Mr. Horn has the knack of stating our problems with the horrifying clarity of a precocious child.

I conclude this Chapter with an extended passage from Stephen Graham's *A Tramp's Sketches*, not only because of its clear links to earlier discussions on Wanderlust, the Lone and Lofty Perch, and to Jim Phelan's description of the tramp as a lost child but also because it showcases Graham's unique prose style. In the following passage, Graham (1913, pp. 258-294) describes the "irreconcilables": "lost children" or "kidnapped persons," those who feel alien everywhere and search in vain for some corner of the world, or universe, that has not been plundered of its mystery:

> I sought them in towns and found them not, for the people ... slumbered and slept. [...] We are many upon the world—we irreconcilables. We cry inconsolably like lost children [...] For perhaps we are kidnapped persons. Perhaps thrones lie vacant on some stars because we are hidden away here upon the earth. [...] we irreconcilable ones; we stand upon many shores and strain our eyes to see into the unknown. We are upon a deserted island and have no boats to take us from star to star, not only upon a deserted island but upon a deserted universe, for even the stars are familiar; they are worlds not unlike our own. The whole universe is our world and it is all explained by the scientists, or is explicable. But beyond the universe, no scientist, not any of us, knows anything. On all shores of the universe washes the ocean of ignorance, the ocean of the inexplicable. We stand upon the confines of an explored world and gaze at many blank horizons. We yearn towards our natural home, the kingdom in which our spirits were begotten. We have rifled the world, and tumbled it upside-down, and run our fingers through all its treasures, yet have not come upon the charter of our birth.

Chapter 6

FACT or FICTION?

As I noted in *The Golden Age of Tramping*, there is a fine line to be drawn between autobiography and fantasy, and so for those obsessed with historical fact—which is for the most part illusory or fabricated anyway—tramp literature is best avoided; unless, that is, one is prepared to fully embrace the autobiographical in fiction and the fictional in autobiography. In any case, even for those who claim they can 'learn' from history, I would argue that myth and legend are equally as instructive, sometimes more so, than so-called historical accounts. Perhaps more importantly, in terms of these vagabond texts, the facts, so far as they *can* be established, are often even more extraordinary than the fiction. Of course, as all fictional writing is born from the mind of an individual's own experiences and interests, it will inevitably contain autobiographical elements, that should go without saying, but the discussion below on vagabond literature takes the fact/fiction argument into an altogether different dimension.

The following tramp writers (all well-read in philosophy, literature and the classics) demonstrate their natural inclination to insert their life and philosophy into their fictional works and fictionalize parts of their autobiographical works; that is the magic of vagabond literature. Furthermore, it is a deception that is often deliberate and unabashed—and in the case of Phelan and Tully, it is also the delight of the Irish blarney. The first two examples, from Kennedy and Tully, discuss part autobiographical works masquerading as fiction.

Bart Kennedy published 22 books and a weekly broadsheet. In *A Man Adrift* and *A Tramp in Spain*, Kennedy is clearly chronicling his own travels and adventures, yet *A Sailor Tramp*, while on the face of it a novel revolving around the adventures of its principal character, Sailor, is clearly heavily informed by the author's own experiences in which he fully exploits both his imagination and his personal philosophy. The lately overused label 'autobiographical fiction' does little justice to what this book represents. On one level, it is an unsentimental essay on the brutality of human life, a critique of deprivation, desperation, and physical and spiritual survival. It also exposes the human face of the tramp, in particular the male tramps' longings and desires, in Sailor's case including that for female companionship.

Attempts have also been made to categorize Jim Tully's 13 books as either autobiography or fiction, but again, this is a somewhat futile exercise. In the case of his third book, *Jarnegan*, although written in the third person, Jack Jarnegan was clearly modeled on Tully in the role of a Hollywood director, yet even his biographers (in spite of the mountain of archives available to them) were unable to reconcile certain facts about Tully from this and other of his works. What we do have from *Jarnegan*, however, is that in describing his hero, Tully gives us an important insight into his own character, one that perfectly fits the description of the cynic vagabond. And it was a derogatory line in *Jarnegan* about his boss, Charlie Chaplin, that lost Tully his job. Ever the cynic *parrhesiast* (his journalistic exposés had earned him the title of "the most feared and hated man in Hollywood"), Tully was given the choice of removing the offending line or losing his job. He chose the latter and, now approaching the peak of his own success, broke up with Chaplin. So clearly were Tully's novels attributable to real-life people and events, that in the case of *Blood on the Moon* (1931, p. 11), he was prompted to make the following remarks:

> While I am immune to the ink-stained bullets of the moral Social Soldiers who carry Truth as a mask, I have thought it best to change names in "Blood on the Moon" to keep them from shooting at those who are my friends. ... If I have not been able to invent a new medium in my picaresque books, I have at least been strong enough not to conform to one that is outworn.

And in the Introduction to that text Tully (1931, p. 12) explains: "I did not study the people in this book as an entomologist does a bug on a pin. I was one of them. I'm still one of them. I can taste the bitterness of their lives in the bread I eat today." Tully's writing simply reflects the writer's attitude to life and his own truth about those he encountered along the way, with no further agenda than to produce a good yarn and achieve prolific book sales.

Jim Phelan was also well aware of what made a successful novel in purely marketing terms and knew just how to please the publishers and readers, while having the last laugh at their expense. As did other tramp writers discussed here, Phelan subverted the commercial with his own skills at storytelling, as he notes in the opening passages of his preface to *The Name's Phelan* (1993, p. i):

> For a teller of tales, a fiction spinner, such as I have been for most of my life, even before I was a writer, any attempt at a straightforward factual narrative is very difficult indeed. It is so easy, and the temptation is so great, to round off a passage or tidy up an episode, to make a neat story instead of the succession of inconsequentialities which a life story usually is. Add the fact that I have always rather tended to dramatise my

own existence, as also that I would much rather forget a great many of the things which have happened to me, and that it will be plain that the ordinary difficulties of autobiography are for me multiplied.

Thomas Manning Page, introduced earlier regarding his time as a bohemian artist, wrote a single volume in the first person without naming himself or other family members, and so there are no clues that the hero of the book was even the author. When commencing a reading of *The Autobiography of a Tramp* (1884, p. 1), in the full belief that Page is both author and narrator, it is easy to be baffled why nothing is given away about where or when Page was born, he simply teases his reader that he was born "in the usual way," at an early age, and from a mother. A cynic par excellence, the satirical irony is there from the book's opening, as Page deliberately defies literary convention by opening his book with a postscript that contains a diatribe against prefaces:

> the custom of writing prefaces is a servile one that has come down to us from those good old days when authors had to choose between the alternatives of starving in garrets or else procuring patronage by fawning like spaniels on such vain, noble personages as were willing to pay for the pleasure of seeing their grand names and mythical virtues embalmed in fulsome print.
>
> When, in the progress of events, it ceased to be necessary to cringe before such beneficence, the literary craftsmen, at a loss by force of habit of something to propitiate, bethought him of the expedient of cringing to the reader; grotesquely ignoring that a book worth the reading needs no apology, and that to a volume of the other sort it is superfluous to add an extenuating which, in the nature of things, is necessarily an enlargement of the offence. (Page, 1884, front matter)

It was only on obtaining a copy of Page's obituary that any 'true facts' concerning the writer could be established. One of these was that he had enrolled in the Confederate Army at the age of 20, serving with some distinction alongside General Robert E. Lee before being wounded several times and eventually released in an exchange of prisoners when the Confederate Army finally surrendered at Appomattox in April 1861. This fact demonstrates the paradoxical, upside-down style of Page's writing and cleared up at least one anomaly: why, one might wonder, did the hero of Page's autobiography, a child soldier in the *Union* army, express so many sympathies with the Southern cause? These deliberate idiosyncrasies of Page's writing are supported in the opening lines of Denis Diderot's *Jacques the Fatalist*, when Diderot (1978, p. 3) highlights the stupidity and pointlessness of seeking out the 'truth' from a story:

HOW HAD THEY MET? BY CHANCE LIKE EVERYONE ELSE. WHAT were their names? What does it matter to you? Whence had they come? From the nearest possible spot. Where were they going? Do we ever know where we're going? What were they saying? The master said nothing, and Jacques said that his captain said that everything that happens to us down here, good or bad, was written up yonder.

Writer Ronald Sukenick concurs with Diderot that the answers to these questions were all written up yonder, getting straight to the point of the conundrum about truth versus fiction when he discusses the most famous of all Western texts, the Bible. Should we regard it as historical fact—incredibly, many apparently sane readers still do—or one of the greatest works of imaginative fiction of the past 2000 years:

> Reality doesn't exist, time doesn't exist, personality doesn't exist. God was the omniscient author, but he died; now no one knows the plot, and since our reality lacks the sanction of a creator, there is no guarantee as to the authenticity of the received version. (Sukenick cited in Federman, 1993, p. 115)

In his third volume *Trader Horn in Madagascar*, Horn (1932, p. 15) tells us: "Beauty of fiction is you can suppress anything that's not convenient." He later describes the book as "fiction buttressed with truth" and that the story was "Founded on as much truth as fiction would allow." The subtitle of his second book, *Harold the Webbed* (1928), includes fictionalizing biographical information that readers normally take for granted:

> ... written by ALFRED ALOYSIUS HORN at the age of seventy-three, and the life with such of his philosophy as is the gift of age and experience, taken down and here edited by ETHELREDA LEWIS.

Horn was, in fact, aged 67, not 73, when the book was published. He deliberately obscures the names of people and places in his writing, and as for dates, he has nothing but contempt: "I've never burdened me memory with dates. A brain's given you for thoughts, not dates." (1932, p. 170):

> dates? ... Excuse me sounding impatient ... When you're here there and everywhere for seventy years you can't be as neat as a lawyer's ledger. A man's got to choose between being a bit o' nature and being chained to the office calendar. (Horn, 1932, p. 204)

Horn would yet have been just another unknown tramp and adventurer had he not arrived, in the spring of 1925 at the age of 64, peddling handmade kitchen implements, at the Johannesburg home of novelist Ethelreda Lewis. Their shared interest in Viking history soon turned into a remarkable literary partnership that, within only two years, would make Horn an international celebrity and, in 1931, spawned the Hollywood movie version of his first book *Trader Horn* (1927). At his weekly visits to Lewis' home, Horn would relate his tales and spend the week writing up his memories in a Johannesburg doss house. Lewis' husband typed up the manuscripts but included all Horn's idiosyncratic grammar and spelling mistakes. The 'conversations' between Horn and Lewis were also included in the final publications, often exceeding Horn's own prose writing. Lewis (cited in Horn, 1932, p. 16) describes Horn's writing as follows:

> Mr. Horn has an enviable gift of speaking as if his characters really existed. The line between truth and fiction is but a shadow line with him. He casts the net of fiction over truth and of truth over fiction, enmeshing the listener by the same dexterous throw.

If Horn had the gift of speaking as though his characters existed, it is because many of them *did* exist. Often modest in his autobiographical ramblings, there is, paradoxically, more truth in much of what he relates than he has been given credit for, or gives himself credit for, including facts that were only verified long after his works were published.

But this literary phenomenon of blurring autobiography and fiction is not confined to tramp writers, the celebrity literary vagabonds discussed by Rickett in his book mirror the delinquency of those discussed above:

> These men believe in the figments of their imagination, and make us believe in them. Stevenson is obviously sceptical as to their reality; we can almost see a furtive smile upon his lip as he writes. But there is nothing unreal about the man, whatever we feel of the Artist. ... there is no make-believe here; here I am not merely amusing myself; here, honestly and heartily admitted, you may find the things that life has taught me."(Rickett, 1906, pp. 122-123)

Rickett's observation that vagabond writers, "believe in the figments of their imagination, and make us believe in them" acknowledges that vagabond writing functions on both a conscious and unconscious level. But as Rickett further notes, the vagabond writer is less concerned with the blurring of fact and fiction than being true to their experiences and observations of life. Something that is directly discussed in Rickett's chapter on George Borrow, at the same time acknowledging the futility (and poor literary technique) of attempting to base autobiography on 'facts':

> the Vagabond is never satisfied with things that merely happen. He is equally concerned with the things that might happen, with the things that ought to happen. And so Borrow added to his own personal record from the storehouse of dreams. Some have blamed him for not adhering to the actual facts. But does any autobiographer adhere to actual facts? Can any man, even with the most sensitive feeling for accuracy, confine himself to a record of what happened?

> Of course not. The moment a man begins to write about himself, to delve in the past, to ransack the storehouse of his memory; then—if he has anything of the literary artist about him, and otherwise his book will not be worth the paper it is written on—he will take in a partner to assist him. That partner's name is Romance. (Rickett, 1906, p. 59)

Rickett quotes directly from Borrow to address the issue head-on, "What is an autobiography? Is it a mere record of a man's life, or is it a picture of the man himself?" This question has been answered by the writer Raymond Federman (1993, p. 93, of whom more below) when he tells us that, "What I finally wrote in my autobiography is not really the story of my life … I have no story, my life is my story. No, the story is my life." Rickett notes that when Borrow started writing up his own life in *Lavengro* he had no intention of departing from the fact: "But the adventurer Vagabond moved uneasily in the guise of the chronicler. He wanted more elbow-room. He remembered all that he hoped to encounter, and from hopes, it was no far cry to actualities."

> Things might have happened so! Ye gods, they did happen so! And after all it matters little to us the exact proportion of fact and fiction. What does matter is that the superstructure he has raised upon the foundation of fact is as strange and unique as the palace of Aladdin. (Rickett, 1906, p. 61)

In *The Thief's Journal*, Jean Genet (1964, p. 61) confirms that, for him, what is written can only ever describe the writer's mindset at the time of writing, not of the period they are attempting to recall.

> We know that our language is incapable of recalling even the pale reflection of those bygone, foreign states. The same would be true of this entire journal if it were to be the notation of what I was. … It is not a quest of time gone by, but a work of art whose pretext-subject is my

former life. It will be a present fixed with the help of the past, and not vice versa.

For the vagabond writer, then, there are no rules or conventions (and certainly no concern for facts) to imprison their imagination when writing. Federman goes even further, suggesting that everything can be said and *must* be said in any possible way and, as with Trader Horn, Jim Phelan and other tramp writers, this included the metafictional approach of writing about the writing process itself.

> While pretending to be telling a story of his life, or the life story of some imaginary being, the surfictionist can at the same time tell the story of the story he is in the process of inventing ... And he can also tell the story of the anguish or joy, disgust or exhilaration he is feeling while writing his story. (Federman, 1993, p. 44)

But to return to Borrow, Rickett discusses what are, on the face of it, contradictory aspects of that writer's character. On the one hand, "the typical Anglo-Saxon in real life," a white-haired giant of six foot three strong, assertive, beer-loving (but never a drunkard), an excellent athlete, "few better at running, jumping, wrestling, sparring, and swimming." On the other hand:

> there was the true Celt whenever he took pen in hand. ... a Celt he was by parentage, and the Celtic part was unmistakable, though below the surface. If the East Anglian in him had a weakness for athleticism, boiled mutton and caper sauce, the Celt in him responded quickly to the romantic associates of Wales. (Rickett, 1906, pp. 60-61)

This characterization of Borrow has many parallels with the lives and writing styles of the tramp writers discussed above, not least Celts Tully and Phelan, fictioneers and pugilists both, and Horn, who claimed a direct descendancy from the Vikings, and whose military tactics he employed in his river battles with pirates on the Ogowe River. Rickett's (1906, pp. 61-62) further comments on Borrows apply equally to these other tramp writers:

> as in all the literary Vagabonds, it is the complexity of the man's temperament that attracts and fascinates. ... a man, in short, of so many bewildering contradictions and strangely assorted qualities as Borrow cannot but compel interest.

A further aspect of vagabond writing, one that should be apparent from many of the passages quoted in this Chapter, is the vagabond writer's link to the Cynic modes of discourse listed in the Introduction. In particular, I wish to emphasize the humor in the writing, discourse that ridicules the object of the writer's satire but often the writer's own self-deprecation also. There is fearlessness (*parrhesia*) as well as mischievousness in delivering the vagabond writer's mockery, as Bart Kennedy (1908, p. 317) acknowledges:

> I often say hard things against the world, but even I must admit that it has a sense of humour. Its humour is a humour that has a bite in it, but better this humour than none at all.

In Jim Tully, we find the true Diogenean Cynic, openly attacking the vain and inglorious, not only in his writing but face to face at Hollywood parties, as noted by his biographers, "puncturing inflated egos with a needle that could take the air out of the room" (Bauer and Dawidziak, 2011, p. 170). Tully assumed the right to say whatever he wanted, in whatever way he wanted, and to hell with people's sensibilities. This process of ridicule has been described by Sloterdijk as "Diogenes' truth test": ridiculing the claims of phonies to see just how much joking they can take, for whoever cannot stand satire directed against them must be false. Not only can truth stand mockery, but it is "freshened by any ironic gesture directed at it" (Sloterdijk, 1988, p. 288). This same characteristic was described by Christopher Stone in his book *Parody* (1914, p. 8):

> ridicule is society's most effective means of curing inelasticity. It explodes the pompous, corrects the well-meaning eccentric, cools the fanatical, and prevents the incompetent from achieving success. Truth will prevail over it, falsehood will cower under it.

FEDERMAN ON TRUTH, FICTION AND LAUGHTER

In his early years at least, the writer Raymond Federman was not a vagabond by choice. At the age of 14, Federman was hastily thrust by his mother into the small upstairs closet of their Paris apartment just before she, his father and two sisters were rounded up by the French police (acting for the Nazis) and taken to Auschwitz where they were killed. After eventually emerging from the closet, the child beat his first train to unoccupied France, surviving on raw potatoes and then later working on a farm, suffering privations and abuse until the war was over. Following his emigration to America, Federman published over 40 works of fiction and memoir (in his case, the two are interchangeable), critical works and poetry. Federman would become a vagabond writer par excellence, deliberately defying every literary convention, including in *Double or Nothing*, writing not only pages with the words reading from bottom to top and right to left, but including a page where every single letter is written backward. *The Voice in the Closet* is a 20-page unpunctuated and uncapitalized sentence revisiting his experience in the closet that saved his life, including how he shits out his fear into a newspaper, wraps the excrement into a package and, before fleeing his hiding place, opens the apartment skylight and deposits the package on the roof. His first action on returning to Paris after the war was to check if the package was still where he left it—it was not.

Another aspect of Federman's writing, already acknowledged in terms of the tramp writers above, is the cynical humor (sometimes tongue in cheek but often biting in its underlying seriousness) that he employed in almost his entire work, whether novelistic or critique—and which also includes self-ridicule and deprecation. Federman coined the term 'laughterature' to describe what, for him, through his writing, was a survival mechanism, a means of making sense of a world he knew to be absurd. How else to make sense of the "unforgivable enormity" of what happened to his family in the Nazi holocaust without going insane other than by ridiculing the absurdity of the event. In *Take It Or Leave It*, one of his longest works—but absent of page numbers—the protagonist, clearly Federman himself (while also speaking of "the other guy," his "storyteller"), considers that other than for the Holocaust, he may have ended his life slaving as a Jewish tailor in Paris. As well as his satirical irony, this extended passage demonstrates Federman's loquaciousness and unstoppable impulse to write outside of the story altogether:

> it's ironical but if that schmuck hitler had guessed that by kicking the hell out of the jews, by wanting to make lamp shades out of them he was going to change the entire structure of the american system, literally change the face of the world, displace the centre of western civilisation, the dumb bastard would have left them alone would have picked another race! Take my case for instance. What do you think I would be? A tailor! Yes a little Jewish tailor Boulevard des Italiens. ... Therefore, funny as it may seem, disturbing and grotesque as it may sound, Hitler in a way was my Savior!
>
> Yes it's laughable! Preposterous!
>
> Go ahead laugh, laugh! I see only an embarrassed smile on your face instead of a big laugh. Don't be shy. I don't give a shit, in fact let's laugh together. ... let's laugh for a good ten or fifteen minutes. It'll relax us in the middle of all that sad stuff. Come on my little friend let's be joyful and take advantage of this situation, especially now that, to be blunt, the scenery round here is rather shitty. I mean in this part of Massachusetts, for have you noticed we are now speeding through Massachusetts ... Therefore let's concentrate on laughter for a while because my dear fellow I'm starting to be fed up with your sad look of a creepy undertaker. Well said! And furthermore the more I think about it the more I am

convinced there is something illegal about your presence here in the middle of my story, some 20 years too soon. How the hell did you manage to pass from the level of the present to the level of the past? (Federman, 1997, Chapter 17, no page numbers)

But the main purpose of including Federman in this Chapter, is that his collection of essays in *Critifiction* is the most thorough and forthright thesis available to argue that ALL writing is fictional, including autobiography and so-called historical accounts, providing a reasoned context for the writing style of all the other vagabonds discussed in this book.

Fiction and autobiography are always interchangeable, just as life and fiction, fact and fiction, language and fiction, that is to say history and the story are interchangeable. And this is because, for me, the STORY always comes first. Or to put it slightly differently: everything is fiction because everything always begins with language, everything is language. The great silence within us must be decoded into words in order to be and to mean. (Federman, 1993, p. 89)

Federman argues that it is the writer's fiction that informs their life, not their life, that determines their fiction: "Paradoxical as it may seem, only fiction is real, only fiction is true. The rest cannot be verified for it remains in the domain of absence". An experience only gains meaning when it is recounted through language. But, Federman (1993, p. 90) further notes, "since language is always deficient and unreliable, the recounting of an experience is also deficient and unreliable." As meaning cannot precede either an experience or language, then meaning can only be deduced from the act of speaking or writing. In this way, he argues, the 'truth' of history can only come after the 'facts' of history and will always be distorted by the telling or writing (Federman, 1993, p. 89).

Similarly with autobiography: "the reader of an autobiography can only believe the words the writer has used, even though he knows that these words are deficient and unreliable." In this way, Federman maintains, autobiographies are always distortions of reality because they are drawn from a memory or an image. This, Federman applies to his entire output of 'surfiction'—the term he coins for his non-critical writing—in which he struggled his whole life to make sense of that life, whether in first, second or third-person narratives. Surfiction, he explains, proliferates from its own substance: "imitating, repeating, echoing, parodying, mocking, re-tracing what it will say. Thus fiction will become a metaphor for its own narrative progress, and will establish and generate itself as it writes" (Federman, 1993, p. 43). Below, Jean Genet (1964, p. 41) emphasizes his own link between writing and creating one's own reality outside of any conventional understanding of autobiography; he freely admits that in creating a journal of his own life—with all the compulsions of the vagabond he is—he entered, in both his life and his writing about his life, into a "fictional aesthetic":

> as a result of a certain frame of mind which is natural to enchantment (being further exalted by my emotion in the presence of nature, endowed with a power recognized by men) I was ready to act, not in accordance with the rules of morality but in accordance with certain laws of a fictional aesthetic ...

In Federman's *Take It Or Leave It*, the narrator and the character frequently shift between first and third-person, changing places. Multiple versions are created in which the 'real' and the fictional Federmans speak to each other. Names, places and dates, deliberately contradict each other to emphasize the fallacy of fact. As in Rickett's comments above, the superstructure the writer raises upon the foundation of facts is, "as strange and unique as the palace of Aladdin", so too, does Federman insist that fact and fiction become secondary to the pleasure of the text. The story must provide satisfaction for its own sake and for the sake of the imagination of both the writer and the reader. To create fiction, Federman says, is to transform reality, even abolish reality, especially abolish the notion that reality is truth. The passage below applies equally to the 'news' and documentaries we absorb daily through the media, as inevitably we, all of us, apply our own imagination to what we read and hear:

> The reality of imagination is more real than reality without imagination, and besides reality as such has never really interested anyone, it is and always has been a form of disenchantment. What makes reality interesting is the imaginary catastrophe that lies behind it. (Federman, 1993, p. 1)

In reading, for example, Trader Horn, one should accept, as Federman suggests, that life and fiction are not distinguishable one from the other, neither is life linear like a novel. One must accept that as life is "always discontinuous and chaotic because it is never experienced in a straight line or an orderly fashion, then similarly linear, chronological, and sequential narration is no longer possible" (Federman, 1993, p. 42). Is this the reason perhaps that Horn introduced the white goddess Nina T into his autobiography (even though she was based on a woman Horn was acquainted with in Central Africa), through his fear that the reader and the publisher needed the pill of a narrative plot to swallow his own chaotic life story. One could equally argue that Horn does not really care what the reader thinks? What is certain, however, is captured perfectly by Lawrence Sterne in *Tristram Shandy* (2017, p. 10) when his hero warns us, "You must have a little patience. I have undertaken, you see, to write not only of my life, but my opinions also." The books of Trader Horn and his fellow storytellers are not for impatient readers.

Chapter 7

THE VAGABOND TEMPERAMENT

In looking back upon these discursive comments on the Vagabond element in modern literature, one cannot help asking what is the resultant effect of the Vagabond temperament upon life and thought. ... Yet the question sooner or later rises to our lips. This Vagabond temperament—is its charm and attractiveness merely superficial? I cannot think so. I think that on the whole its effect upon our literature has been salutary and beneficial.

Arthur Rickett (1906, p. 15)

Rickett's chapter on Robert Louis Stevenson provides particular insight into answering these questions. He refers to two aspects of Stevenson's character, which he describes as the controlling forces of that writer's nature, the Romantic and the Artistic:

> It may be thought that these twain have much in common; but it is not so. In poetry the first gives us a Blake, a Shelley; the second a Keats, a Tennyson. Variety, fresh points of view, these are the breath of life to the Romantic. But for the Artist there is one constant, unchanging ideal. The Romantic ventures out of sheer love of the venture, the other out of sheer love for some definite end in view. It is not usual to find them coexisting as they did in Stevenson, and their dual existence gives an added piquancy and interest to his work. It is the Vagabond Romantic in him that leads him into so many byways and secret places, that sends him airily dancing over the wide fields of literature; ever on the move, making no tabernacle for himself in any one grove. And it is the Artist who gives that delicacy of finish, that exquisite nicety of touch, to the veriest trifle that he essays. The matter may be beggarly, the manner is princely.
>
> [...]
>
> And thus it is that in the letters alone do we find the Vagabond temperament of Stevenson fully asserting itself. ... He does not care a fig for order, or logical sequence, or congruity, or for striking a key of expression and keeping it, but becomes simply the most spontaneous and unstudied of human beings. He will write with the most

distinguished eloquence on one day, with simple good sense and good feeling on a second, with flat triviality on another, and with the most slashing, often ultra-colloquial vehemency on a fourth, or will vary through all these moods, and more, in one and the same letter. (Rickett, 1906, pp. 123-125)

In Stevenson, then, we find the same vagabond characteristics as those in less well-known tramp writers, both in his temperament and his writing. He responds to internal humors and desires, not to societal pressures and expectations. Rickett lists three characteristics that he finds in the vagabond temperament, and these apply equally to the tramp writers discussed in my own study:

(1) Restlessness—the wandering instinct; this expresses itself mentally as well as physically. (2) A passion for the Earth—shown not only in the love of the open air, but in a delight in all manifestations of life. (3) A constitutional reserve whereby the Vagabond, though rejoicing in the company of a few kindred souls, is put out of touch with the majority of men and women. (Rickett, 1906, p. 8)

In Rickett's chapter on Henry D. Thoreau, we get closer to precisely what it is that puts the vagabond out of touch 'with the majority of men and women,' and this has more to do with a rejection of wider society's norms and values than it does a 'constitutional reserve.' "May not Thoreau's energetic rebukes of the evils of civilisation have received an added zest from his instinctive repugnance to many of the civilised amenities valued by the majority?" (Rickett, 1906, p. 107)

A few days before his twenty-eighth birthday, Thoreau went to live alone for over two years in a cabin in the woods on the shores of Walden Pond, a mile from the nearest neighbor—even if that neighbor was his mother, where he had regular meals and his laundry taken care of. This does not detract, though, from his writing and commentary on the subject under discussion. Rickett informs us that Thoreau was exceptionally practical and skilled at everything "from making lead pencils to constructing a boat" to the extent that, "had he been so disposed he could doubtless have made a fortune". We are also told that he supported himself with manual labor throughout his life. Thoreau's writing is full of attacks on the evils of money-making and 'civilisation' in general. Yet Thoreau's escape to Walden Pond was more than simply a negative response to wider society's evils, an "escape from ordinary life", he rather saw it as a positive lifestyle choice, a natural way of fitting himself *into* an ordinary life. Rickett credits much of Thoreau's lifestyle to his sympathy with the Native American and his knowledge of their ways, a characteristic shared with other vagabond writers:

> The Indians were to Thoreau what the gypsies were to Borrow. Appealing to certain spiritual affinities in the men's natures, they revealed their own temperaments to them, enabling them to see the distinctiveness of their powers. (Rickett, 1906, p. 97)

That certain vagabond writers were drawn to those who lived on the margins of mainstream society and also embraced 'foreign' cultures that complemented their own nature, has been a recurring theme for over two and a half thousand years going back to the mythical vagabond Heracles and questioning the very nature of 'civilization' itself:

> We talk of civilizing the Indians, but that is not the name for his improvement. By the wary independence and aloofness of his dim forest-life he preserves his intercourse with his native gods, and is admitted from time to time to a rare and peculiar society with Nature. [...]
>
> If one could listen but for an instant to the chant of the Indian muse, we should understand why he will not exchange his savageness for civilization. Nations are not whimsical. Steel and blankets are strong temptations, but the Indian does well to continue Indian. (Thoreau, cited in Rickett, 1906, pp. 99-100)

Rickett acknowledges that the life of the woods came naturally to Thoreau because he, "had a sufficient touch of wildness to be able to detach himself from the civilized man's point of view." Thoreau passed by indifferently, Rickett says, the luxuries and aspirations that mean so much to those who embrace mainstream society. As with the Cynic Crates, who created his own republic from his immediate friends and family and recognized that man-made laws were at odds with the natural laws of human nature, so to did Thoreau maintain his own integrity "through obedience to the laws of his own being" (Rickett, 1906, p. 101).

A historical example of the vagabond's tendency to find a natural existence with the marginalized of society was the Cynosarges (Park of the Agile Dog). The Cynosarges was a gymnasium and a temple to the worship of the proto-Cynic Heracles, located just outside the walls of Athens. Traceable to the sixth century B.C., the Cynosarges was the only place where Athenian 'bastards' were permitted to worship and exercise. Bastards were defined by Athenian law as including anyone with an Athenian father but whose mother was a slave, a prostitute, or a foreigner, as well as those whose parents were not legally married citizens. Generally well assimilated into Athenian life, a law passed in the fifth century B.C. prohibited bastards from exercising in the gymnasiums. For some reason, this law did not extend to the Cynosarges, which thus became a regular gathering place, not only for official bastards, but also self-proclaimed bastards: "men and women who were or felt illegitimate and foreign everywhere, and who lived ill at ease within the established civic community" (Navia, 1996, p. 16).

The vagabond and cynic philosopher would have us *live* our philosophy, the knowledge and wisdom that comes from hard living, rather than from the books and teachings of 'experts.' This is the essence of vagabondage, a reconnection to our natural surroundings, trusting only the knowledge that we receive through our own senses, as opposed to academic, scientific knowledge and its belief in first principles and external absolutes—the mindset that has dominated Western thought for over two thousand years.

Recapping then on the main characteristics of the vagabond writers' temperament. First and foremost, the vagabond is an individual, not concerned with being part of any movement or persuading others to their point of view, they are marked out by their unique imagination and 'old-fashioned' habits of thought. Their primary goal is the absence of monotony, partially achieved by not having to follow planned events and divesting themselves of the artificiality, which they are convinced is the lot of their fellow humans. Rather than seeking to change the world around them—which, in any case, they know to be chaotic and *beyond* human control—they rather seek to maximize their own life here on earth. In this way, the vagabond enters into a new relationship with the world, becoming a creature of the moment and adopting a philosophy influenced by the natural world in which they come into contact, clear of all ties to conventional, mannered living. In their day-to-day life, they ignore state boundaries and man-made laws, escaping the suffocating glue of mainstream society's rules and conventions. As already noted by Nietzsche above (1909, p. 25): "It is so provincial to bind oneself to views which are no longer binding a couple of hundred miles away," and in this sense, the vagabond becomes a cosmopolite, a citizen of the world. Even if the vagabond has a regular home, they are born with a vagrant strain in the blood and, particularly when young, are frequently on the move carrying the minimum possessions to get by. Their passion for the Earth, their affinity with the natural world, and their understanding of the healthy desires experienced by animals, guides their lifestyle and their attitude to the rest of the human herd. This can be perceived as an aloofness and personal detachment which, although marking the vagabond out from regular humanity, for the most part, comes from a genuine concern for those he or she believes could and should do better.

Finally, being young at heart and avoiding an orthodox education, can give the vagabond the persona of the child who never grows old.

As for whether one is born with or develops such a temperament, I do believe, from all the texts I have read, that one cannot simply become a vagabond—a vagabond in the sense described in this book. The spirit must be 'in the blood,' giving rise to the irresistible urges that both plague and pleasure the vagabond in equal measure. As for the vagabond writer, they may have all railed against a formal education, but, in most cases, they needed access to a certain level of formal knowledge and literary support to be able to get their works written and published. I will end this little book by thanking them all for doing just that and for the pleasure and knowledge they have afforded me in coming to understand this much-neglected philosophy of life—standing outside of conventional learning as it does—a little better.

REFERENCES

Abbs, Annabel. (2021) *Wind Swept: why women walk*, London: Two Roads Books.

Andrews, Kerri. (2020) *Wanderers: A History of Women Walking*, London: Reaktion Books Ltd. Reproduced with permission of the Licensor through PLSclear.

Bakhtin, Mikhail. (1999) *Problems of Dostoevesky's Poetics*, Minneapolis: University of Minnesota Press.

Bauer, Paul and Dawidziak, Mark. (2011) *Jim Tully: American Writer, Irish Rover and Hollywood Brawler*, Kent State University Press.

Baudelaire, Charles. (1964) *The Painter of Modern Life and Other Essays*, London: Phaidon Press Limited.

Beckett, Samuel. (1980) *The Expelled and other Novellas*, London: Penguin Books.

Belloc, Hilaire (intro). (1911) *The Footpath Way: an anthology for walkers*, London: Sidgewick & Jackson Ltd.

Benjamin, Walter. (2002) *The Arcades Project*, Harvard University Press.

Bettenson, Henry, (ed.) (1990) *The Early Christian Fathers: A selection from the writings of the Fathers from St. Clement of Rome to St. Athanasius*, Oxford University Press.

Bewes, Timothy. (1997) *Cynicism and Postmodernity*, London: Verso.

Branham, R. Bracht. (1996) 'Intro', in Branham R. Bracht & Marie- Odile Goulet-Caze (ed's), *The Cynics: The Cynic Movement in Antiquity and Its Legacy*, Berkeley: University of California Press. https://doi.org/10.1525/97805 20921986

Burbank, Emily M. (1908) 'Josiah Flynt—An Impression,' in Flynt, Josiah., *My Life*, New York: The Outing Publishing Company.

Burroughs, John. (1911) 'The Exhilarations of the Road,' in Belloc, Hilaire., *The Footpath Way: an anthology for walkers*, London: Sidgewick & Jackson Ltd.

Cendrars, Blaise. (2004) The Astonished Man, London: Peter Owen.

Chickena, Hib, and Kat, Kika. (2003) *Off the Map*, CrimethInc.

Christy, Jim. (2025) *Keep on Working*, Victoria (British Columbia): Ekstasis Editions.

Christy, Jim. (2012) *Jackpots*, Victoria BC: Ekstasis Editions.

Christy, Jim. (n.d) *Wandering Heart*, unpublished manuscript.

Chrysostom, Dio. (2012) *6th Oration*, cited in Dobbin, Robert (translator, editor). *The Cynic Philosophers from Diogenes to Julian*, London: Penguin Classics.

Clébert, Jean-Paul. (2016) *Paris Vagabond*, New York: New York Review of Books.

Clébert, Jean-Paul. (1964) *The Gypsies*, London: Readers Union, Cresswell, Tim., *The Tramp in America*, London: Reaction Books, 2001.

Cutler, Ian. (2005) *Cynicism from Diogenes to Dilbert*, Jefferson (NC): McFarland & Company, Inc. Reproduced with permission of McFarland & Company, Inc., Box 611, Jefferson NC 28640. www. mcfarlandbooks.com.

Cutler, Ian. (2019) *Jim Christy: A Vagabond Life*, Port Townsend (WA): Feral House.

Cutler, Ian. (2020) *The Lives And Extraordinary Adventures Of Fifteen Tramp Writers From The Golden Age Of Vagabondage*, Port Townsend (WAS): Feral House.

Cutler, Ian. (2010) 'A Tale of Two Cynics: the philosophic duel between Jesus and the woman from Syrophoenicia,' *The Philosophical Forum, Inc.*, Vol. XLI, No. 4, Winter. https://doi.org/10.1111/j.1467-9191.2010.00369.x

Davies, William Henry. (2013) *The Autobiography of a Super-Tramp*, Pwllheli (Wales): Cromen.

Debord, Guy. (1955) 'Introduction to a Critique of Urban Geography' in *Les Lèvres Nues* #6, September.

DePastino, Todd. (2003) *Citizen Hobo: how a century of homelessness shaped America*, University of Chicago Press. https://doi.org/10.7208/chicago/9780226143804.001.0001

Dickens, Charles. (1905) *The Uncommercial Traveller*, London: Chapman & Hall Ltd.

Diderot, Denis. (1978) *Jacques the Fatalist and his Master*, New York: Norton.

Diderot, Denis. (2018) *Philosophical Thoughts and Other Texts*, Independently published.

Dobbin, Robert (translator, editor). (2012) *The Cynic Philosophers from Diogenes to Julian*, London: Penguin Classics.

Downing, F. Gerald. (1992) *Cynics and Christian Origins*, Edinburgh: T&T Clark.

Dudley, D. R. (1937) *A History of Cynicism: From Diogenes to the 6th Century AD*, London: Methuen & Co. Ltd.

Ehrman, Bart D. (ed.) (2003) *Lost Scriptures: books that did not make it into the New Testament*, Oxford University Press Inc.

Federman, Raymond. (1993) *Critifiction*, Albany: State University of New York Press.

Federman, Raymond. (1997) *Take It Or Leave It*, Illinois State University Press: FC2.

Federman, Raymond. (2000) *The Twofold Vibration*, Los Angeles: Green Integer.

Ferrell, Jeff. (2018) *Drift: Illicit Mobility and Uncertain Knowledge*, Oakland: University of California Press. https://doi.org/10.1525/california/9780520295544.001.0001

Flynt, Josiah. (1901) *Tramping with Tramps: Studies and Sketches of Vagabond Life*, New York: The Century Co.

Flynt, Josiah. (1908) *My Life*, New York: The Outing Publishing Company.

Flynt, Josiah. (1927) 'Homosexuality Among Tramps,' Appendix A in Havelock Ellis, *Studies in the Psychology of Sex*, Volume 2, Sexual Inversion, Philadelphia: F.A. Davis Company.

Genet, Jean. (1964) *The Thief's Journal*, New York: Bantam Books.

Graham, Stephen. (1913) *A Tramp's Sketches*, London: MacMillan & Co.

Graham, Stephen. (1926) *The Gentle Art of Tramping*, New York: D. Appleton & Company.
Graham, Stephen. (1929) *London Nights*, London: The Bodley Head Ltd.
Harper, Douglas. (1882) *Good Company*, University of Chicago Press.
Hazlitt, William. (1822) 'On Going a Journey,' *The New Monthly Magazine and Literary Journal*, January.
Hickman, Katie. (2022) *Brave Hearted: The Dramatic Story of Women of the American West*, London: Virago.
Horn, Trader. (1928) *Harold the Webbed or The Young Vykings* [sic], New York: Simon and Schuster.
Horn, Trader. (1932) *Trader Horn in Madagascar: The Waters of Africa*, London: Jonathan Cape.
Illich, Ivan. (1974) *Limits to Medicine: Medical Nemesis—The Expropriation of Health*, London: Marion Boyars. https://doi.org/10.1016/S0140-6736(74)90361-4
Julian, Roman emperor. (2012) cited in Dobbin, Robert (translator, editor), *The Cynic Philosophers from Diogenes to Julian*, London: Penguin Classics.
Kennedy, Bart. (1900) *A Man Adrift*, Chicago: Herbert S. Stone & Company.
Kennedy, Bart. (1902) *A Sailor Tramp*, London: George Newnes Ltd.
Kennedy, Bart. (1908) *A Tramp's Philosophy*, London: John Long.
Kerouac, Jack. (1960) 'The Vanishing American Hobo' in *Holiday Magazine* (Philadelphia, PA), Vol. 27, No. 3, March.
Kristeva, Julia. (1982) *Powers of Horror: an essay on abjection*, New York: Columbia University Press.
Lacan, Jacques. cited by Botting, Fred. & Wilson, Scott. (2001) *Bataille*, Basingstoke: Palgrave.
Laërtius, Diogenes. (1995) *Lives of Eminent Philosophers, Vol II*, Cambridge (Mass): Harvard University Press.
Laing, Olivia. (2021) *Everybody: A Book About Freedom*, London: Picador.
Langley, Bob. (1977) *Lobo: A Vagabond in America*, London: Robert Hale Ltd.
Livingston, Leon Ray. (1912) *The Curse of Tramp Life*, Cambridge Springs, PA: A-No. 1 Publishing Co.
London, Jack. (1903) *People of the Abyss*, Edinburgh: Thomas Nelson and Sons Ltd.
London, Jack. (1907) *The Road*, New York: Macmillan.
Lucian. (1996) The Passing of Peregrinus', in *Lucian Volume V*, Loeb Classical Library, Cambridge (Mass): Harvard University Press.
Malherbe, Abraham J. (1977) *The Cynic Epistles*, Atlanta: Scholars Press.
Martineau, Harriet. (1838) *How to Observe Morals and Manners*, London: Charles Knight and Co.
Maté, Gabor. (2024) *The Myth of Normal: Illness, health & healing in a toxic culture*, London: Penguin/Random House.
McFee, William (Foreword), cited in Horn, Alfred Aloysius. (2002) *Trader Horn: A Young Man's Outstanding Adventures in 19th Century Equatorial Africa*, San Francisco: Traveler's Tales' Classics.

McIntyre, Iain (Ed.). (2018) *On the Fly! Hobo Literature and Songs 1879-1941*, Oakland (CA): PM Press.

Miller, Henry. (2001) *Tropic of Cancer*, London: Harper Collins.

Murray, Alison. (2000) *Train on the Brain*, Channel 4/TVO documentary.

Navia, Luis E. (1996) *Classical Cynicism: a critical study*, Connecticut: Greenwood Press. https://doi.org/10.5040/9798400627255

Navia, Luis E. (1998) *Diogenes of Sinope: the man in the tub*, New York: Greenwood Press.

Navia, Luis E. (2001) *Antisthenes of Athens: setting the world aright*, New York: Greenwood Press.

Niehues-Probsting, Heinrich., 'The Modern Reception of Cynicism: Diogenes in the Enlightenment,' in R. Bracht Branham & Marie-Odile Goulet-Caze (ed's) (1996) *The Cynics: The Cynic Movement in Antiquity and Its Legacy*, Berkeley: University of California Press. https://doi.org/10.1525/9780520921986-016

Nietzsche, Friedrich. (1909) *Beyond Good and Evil: prelude to a philosophy of the future*, in *Complete Works, Volume Five*, Edinburgh: T.N. Foulis.

Nietzsche, Friedrich. (1909) *Thoughts out of Season*, Part II, in *Complete Works*, London: George Allen & Unwin.

Nietzsche, Friedrich. (1992) *Ecce Homo: how one becomes what one is*, London: Penguin Books.

Nietzsche, Friedrich. (1999) *The Anti-Christ*, Tucson: See Sharp Press.

Nietzsche, Friedrich. (1997) *Twilight of the Idols: or, how to philosophize with the hammer*, Indianapolis: Hackett Publishing Co. Inc.

Orwell, George. (2021) *Down and Out in Paris and London*, London: Harper Collins.

Oxford Bibliographies (online) (2023) Oxford University Press.

Page, Thomas Manning. (1884) *Bohemian Life; or The Autobiography of a Tramp*, St. Louis: Sun Publishing Company.

Phelan, Jim. (1955) *Tramping the Toby*, London: Burke Publishing Co. Ltd.

Phelan, Jim. (1993) *The Name's Phelan*, Belfast: Blackstaff Press Ltd.

Phelan, Kathleen. (1972) 'I am a Vagabond,' *Woman's Own*.

Rickett, Arthur. (1906) *The Vagabond in Literature*, London: J. M. Dent & Co.

Roberts, Morley. (1904) *A Tramp's Note-Book*, London: F. V. White & Co. Ltd.

Rose, Margaret A. (1993) *Parody: Ancient, Modern, & Postmodern*, Cambridge, Cambridge University Press.

Sante, Luc. (2015) *The Other Paris*, New York: Farrar, Straus and Giroux.

Sayre, Farrand. (1938) *Diogenes of Synope: A Study of Greek Cynicism*, Baltimore: J.H.Furst Co.

Scott, Sir Walter., 'A Strolling Pedlar,' cited in Belloc, Hilaire. (1911) *The Footpath Way: an anthology for walkers*, London: Sidgewick & Jackson Ltd.

Sebald, W. G. (1998) *The Rings of Saturn*, New York: New Directions.

Sharples, R. W. (1996) *Stoics, Epicureans and Sceptics*, London: Routledge.

Sloterdijk, Peter. (1988) *Critique of Cynical Reason*, London: Verso.

REFERENCES

Smith, Sydney. 'Walking an Antidote to City Poison,' cited in Belloc, Hilaire. (1911) *The Footpath Way: an anthology for walkers*, London: Sidgewick & Jackson Ltd.

Solnit, Rebecca. (2001) *Wanderlust: A History of Walking*, London: Verso.

Stephen, Leslie. 'In Praise of Walking,' cited in Belloc, Hilaire. (1911) *The Footpath Way: an anthology for walkers*, London: Sidgewick & Jackson Ltd.

Sterne, Lawrence. (2017) *The Life and Opinions of Tristram Shandy, Gentleman*, Richmond (Surry): Alma Classics.

Stevenson, R. L. (1876) 'Walking Tours', *Cornhill Magazine*, Vol, 33.

Stevenson, R. L. (1904) *An Inland Voyage*, London: Chatto & Windus.

Stevenson, R. L. (1905) *Essays on Travel*, London: Chatto & Windus.

Stevenson, R. L. (2022) *Travels with a Donkey in the Cevennes & Other Travel Writing*, Moncreiffe Press.

Stone, Christopher. (1914) *Parody*, London: M. Secker.

Thoreau, H. D., 'Walking, and the Wild', in Belloc, Hilaire. (1911) *The Footpath Way: an anthology for walkers*, London: Sidgewick & Jackson Ltd.

Tully, Jim. (1926) *Jarnegan*, New York: Albert & Charles Boni.

Tully, Jim. (1931) *Blood on the Moon*, New York: Coward-McCann.

Walser, Robert. (1992) *The Walk*, London: Serpent's Tail.

Wickes, George. (1974) *Henry Miller Down and out in Paris*, London: Village Press.

Woolf, Virginia. (1930) *Street Haunting*, San Francisco: The Westgate Press.

Woolf, Virginia. (1975) *The Flight of Mind: The Letters of Virginia Woolf, Volume One*, London: The Hogarth Press.

Woolf, Virginia. (1980) *The Diary of Virginia Woolf, Volume II 1920-1924*, New York: Harcourt Brace Jovanovich.

Woolf, Virginia. (1982) *The Diary of Virginia Woolf, Volume IV 1931-1935*, London: Hogarth Press.

Yancey, Dolly Kennedy. (1909) *The Tramp Woman*, St Louis: Britt Publishing Company.

www.ingramcontent.com/pod-product-compliance
Lightning Source LLC
Chambersburg PA
CBHW061419300426
44114CB00015B/1987